new natural
Thames & Hudson

home

With 386 illustrations, 340 in color

Dominic Bradbury Photographs by Richard Powers

To Maximilian, Mia, Florence, Cecily and Noah

Dominic Bradbury and Richard Powers would like to express their sincere gratitude to the many owners and architects of the houses featured in this book for all of their generous help and support. Special thanks to Lucas Dietrich, Jennie Condell, Cat Glover, Anna Perotti, Rowena Stanyer and all at Thames & Hudson, along with Gordon Wise and Shaheeda Sabir at Curtis Brown.

Page 1 Andrzej Zarzycki's self-designed house in the New Forest, UK
Pages 2–3 The Wabi House, CA, by Sebastian Marsical Studio (see page 54)
Pages 4–5 The Utzon Cabin by Kim Utzon, Tibirke, Denmark (see page 152)

First published in 2011 in hardcover in the United States of America by Thames & Hudson Inc., 500 Fifth Avenue, New York, New York 10110

thamesandhudsonusa.com

Library of Congress Catalog Card Number 2010936236

ISBN 978-0-500-51561-7

Printed and bound in China by Imago

The **new natural home** offers a better way of living in every sense. It is a house that is **thoughtfully designed** and **sensitively built**, while its low energy use makes it cheaper to run day by day. It is **flexible**, **functional** and **adaptable** so that it will **evolve** and **change** with our families. New natural homes are **practical**, **long-lasting** and **hard-wearing** on the one hand, and **beautiful** and **aesthetically seductive** on the other. They **respect the landscape** and the environment, while forming the most **enticing of picture frames** to the world outside. They have something for every single one of us.

introduction
building better homes

Inspiring Change

We know that the planet needs more than a little tenderness and care. We realize that we have to start changing the way we live so as to help the environment and help ourselves. We should also know by now that house and home are at the very forefront of a green revolution that will ultimately change the way our most personal retreats are designed and ordered.

A house is, of course, a very special kind of building that forms the backdrop to a significant part of our daily lives. It is a highly personal haven from which we demand an extraordinary amount. This is a place for rest and relaxation, entertaining and gathering together, but increasingly it is also a place of work and study. A house has to be extremely hard-working in itself: a space where we need to be able to function efficiently and easily, whether we are cooking a meal, doing our laundry or bathing and exercising. It is also a key platform for consumption in every sense, from the very building blocks that make up the structure of our home to the energy used to run it day to day, as well as the endless foods and products that regularly pass through it.

At heart, we understand the critical importance of our homes in the struggle against climate change. We have moved beyond the need for lectures, guilt trips and documentaries and are now going about the business of making a difference. Most of all, we are looking for inspiration.

'We need to give consumers something where they can see that the future is not going to be hell or all about living in recycled clay houses,' says designer Christoph Behling, a pioneer in applied solar technology and building, as well as a product creator for luxury brands such as Tag Heuer. 'The future will work for us and there will be moments of joy and pleasure. Above all, we need to get away from the word *alternative*, as in *alternative living*, and the idea that it means that we will have to make do with something slightly less good or less pleasant. If we aim for alternative, then we will fail. We don't get out of bed for alternative. We get out of bed for better, nicer, happier.'

Inspiring change will be key to the success of the green revolution, which will ultimately become every bit as profound as the Modernist architectural revolution of the twentieth century. In the early days of the green movement there was this hair-shirt idea that we would have to compromise and make do, that we would have to let go of all sorts of luxuries we had grown used to and live in houses made of straw.

But the reality is that we should simply be aiming for better homes in every sense: houses that are better designed and built, that use less energy and are cheaper to run, that are more flexible and adaptable,

We have moved beyond the need for lectures, guilt trips and documentaries and are now going about the business of making a difference.

The design and creation of a house is both a practical process and an artistic, creative undertaking.... It is a highly intense process that demands sensitivity, a huge amount of thought and a lot of common sense.

Previous pages The Tinbeerwah House in Noosa, Australia, by Bark Design, makes the most of its rich natural setting among the eucalyptus trees, with views over the woodlands to the Pacific Ocean.

Above and opposite Richard Neutra's Kaufmann Desert House (Palm Springs, CA, 1946) and Frank Lloyd Wright's Fallingwater (Bear Run, PA, 1935) famously celebrate strong connections with their dramatic natural settings and develop key relationships between indoor and outdoor living.

that will evolve and change as our families evolve and change. They will also be practical, long-lasting and hard-wearing on the one hand, beautiful and aesthetically seductive on the other. The materials from which they are made will be as environmentally low-impact as possible, and the buildings themselves will respect their sites, contexts and surroundings. This is not about making do, but about making our houses better for ourselves and for our families, while taking a sensitive and common sense approach to the environment.

Balancing Acts

The design and creation of a house is both a practical process and an artistic, creative undertaking. It is also a highly intricate balancing act in the course of which so many different questions have to be asked and answered, from the choice of foundation to the coating on the roof, from the skin wrapped around the house to a decision about taps for the kitchen sink. It is a highly intense process that demands sensitivity, a huge amount of thought and a lot of common sense.

Given all this complexity, perhaps it is not so surprising that somewhere around the second half of the twentieth century we lost our way when it came to home architecture. In the rush to build volume houses and housing, architects and developers often created buildings that were desperately inadequate and poorly conceived and constructed. These were little more than disposable structures that would not last much longer than a car and then need pulling down and replacing, with all the vast amounts of energy and waste involved.

At the same time, we found ourselves talking about 'sick-building syndrome' as we realized that hermetically sealed houses and offices were susceptible to health-damaging build-ups of carbon dioxide as well as toxins from man-made paints, furniture and plastics.

It was as though common sense had been forgotten along with the lessons of traditional and vernacular buildings – barns to farmsteads to cottages and townhouses – that had been around for centuries while successfully adapting to changing patterns of life and living. The complex balancing act behind the design and build of each and every home was becoming corrupted.

At the same time, the impact of such construction and waste on the environment was – and still is – absolutely vast. Statistics are hard to pin down and so often arguable, but the total global construction industry could be responsible for as much as 40 per cent of worldwide carbon dioxide emissions, solid waste and energy use. The production of cement – the active ingredient in concrete – is thought to be responsible for somewhere between 5 and 8 per cent of global CO_2 emissions alone. In America, home energy use – largely for heating and cooling – accounts for at least 20 per cent of total greenhouse-gas emissions. In the UK, as much as half of all CO_2 emissions come from lighting and heating buildings, including our houses.

So the idea of simply tearing down and replacing dysfunctional buildings that are only twenty or thirty years old is frightening on many levels, with all of that wasted energy and the mass of rubble and rubbish to be disposed of, much of it heading for landfill. This is especially worrying given that the recycling industry is still desperately struggling to catch up with the great volume of waste produced every single day.

Now, though, we are entering a new phase in which we can start to be more optimistic that this kind of reckless design and waste will become more and more limited. The green agenda has now become important enough to push right into the heart of the whole design and build process.

Past and Future

Traditional and vernacular homes have a great deal to teach us about designing the homes of the future. Significant building stock from the eighteenth and nineteenth centuries and earlier has not only lasted and survived, but has also adapted well to twentieth- and twenty-first-century living. This ideal of a home that both endures and adapts is vital in itself to the future of the sustainable home, as we move away from the bankrupt concept of short-shelf-life building.

Given the amount of embodied energy that goes into any building – not to mention the effort, work and creativity – we must return to the idea of a house that lasts for centuries and not decades and that can adapt to the needs of different owners and generations. This is a shift away from the mindset that has come to see the house as a temporary presence on a far more valuable site ripe for redevelopment.

Many of the great Modernist pioneers were acutely aware of the lessons and examples of architectural history, even as they forged a new way to approach design. One thinks of Frank Lloyd Wright, for instance, who emerged out of the Arts and Crafts Movement, which placed such emphasis on natural and carefully crafted materials. Wright was a great advocate of 'organic design', emphasizing the need for houses and buildings that responded to their sites and surroundings, emerging as a direct and considered response to them. The term also drew on the idea that a piece of architecture should work as a collective and cohesive whole rather than as a series of components, reflecting the symbiotic relationships seen in the natural world.

Wright's Fallingwater (1935), most famously, is intimately connected to its setting, woven into the existing rugged landscape of Bear Run, Pennsylvania, with its stream flowing under cantilevered platforms and terraces. The house respects the setting rather than seeking to impose itself on the landscape, recognizing that the relationship between architecture and setting is of vital significance, especially in such a unique natural environment.

Richard Neutra – one of the great experimental American West Coast Modernists – also stressed the importance of the relationship between client and nature within the design of a whole series of landmark houses, from the Lovell Health House (1929) in Los Angeles to the Kaufmann Desert House (1946) in Palm Springs. He coined the concept of biorealism to sum up his approach to integrating home and setting, establishing a fluid relationship between exterior and interior living spaces and inviting the landscape into the house.

The Kaufmann Desert House makes the most of its powerful setting, with views of the surrounding mountains. A 'gloriette' – an outdoor living room – on the roof makes for an extraordinary semi-sheltered viewing deck, while the glass walls of the main open-plan living spaces on the ground floor retract to allow a seamless progression to the terraces, pool and gardens. Neutra argued that the architecture of the home was a key ingredient of well-being and healthy living, using elements such as pools and planting to promote a sense of connection to the natural world.

Other California Modernists such as Rudolph Schindler and Albert Frey also explored the borderland between indoor and outdoor living, creating a new and more informal paradigm, while Pierre Koenig explored ways of naturally venting

and cooling his buildings, so avoiding the need for air conditioning. In Mexico, Luis Barragán – among the most accomplished of regional Modernists – also worked in concert with nature and sunlight as he sought to reinvent the colonial haciendas of the past for a new age, seen to most powerful effect in his designs for the horse ranch of Cuadra San Cristóbal (1968) near Mexico City.

The great Scandinavian Alvar Aalto pioneered a softer and more seductive version of Modernist architecture, with houses such as Villa Mairea (1939) at Noormarkku in Finland. Here the surrounding forests seem to seep into the house itself, with its richly textured timber finishes and supporting pillars echoing the countless tree trunks of the nearby countryside. Aalto emphasized context, natural materials and framed views of the landscape. He was also – like Neutra – acutely aware of the impact design and architecture could have on an individual's health and state of mind.

In many respects, these masters were the forebears of a fresh breed of contemporary architects who are also trying to combine respect for the natural world and the environment with a push towards a more dynamic approach to the design of the sustainable contemporary home. More widely, we are all having to relearn some of the lessons laid down by the likes of Wright and Aalto as we look to them – along with today's pioneers – for inspiration.

Green Dreams

There are, of course, many contemporary architects working with green ideas and sustainability in mind and whose work is inspirational. This book features a number of them. These are architects from around the world whose houses are unique and considered responses to specific sites, surroundings and contexts.

Certainly, the idea of site-specific and contextual architecture has to be one key element within the evolution of the truly green modern home. There is no one-size-fits-all solution to the challenge of designing a sustainable contemporary house, and even prefabricated designs will – at their best – have a level of flexibility that allows a design to be tailored to a specific site or position. The sustainable home is one that allows itself to be successfully orientated to take best advantage of natural conditions, taking into account important concerns such as solar gain, natural light and cross-ventilation. At the same time, the new natural home will also draw on locally available materials, such as regionally sourced timber or stone.

Australian architect Glenn Murcutt is one architect who has been making such concerns an intrinsic part of his work for decades. Although staying true to his Australian roots and remaining a sole practitioner, Murcutt has become an international figurehead for architects and designers interested in questions of sustainability and contextuality.

Murcutt's work – especially his country houses, such as the Simpson-Lee House (1994) in Mount Wilson, or the Marie Short House in Kempsey (see page 102) – adhere to the Aboriginal maxim of 'touching the earth lightly'. They are careful responses to particular conditions and climates, which can vary widely across the vast territory of

Left Contemporary versions of the recreation deck by Bark Design (Noosa, Australia) and Lundberg Design (Sonoma County, CA) create enticing viewing platforms, as well as zones for relaxation and bathing.

Opposite At the house Harry Seidler built for his mother, Rose, at Wahroonga, NSW, Australia, in 1950, an integrated terrace on the upper level brings sunlight into the heart of the building and offers dramatic views out across the landscape.

Australia. The designs of Murcutt's houses take sensitive account of the passage of the sun, the movement of the wind and the need to relate a building to the landscape. At the same time, he tends to use local materials – for example, eucalyptus timber in the case of the Marie Short House – and local craftspeople. But none of this comes at the expense of originality or beauty. 'I cannot pursue my architecture without considering the minimization of energy consumption, simple and direct technologies, a respect for site, climate, place and culture,' Murcutt stated in his 2002 Pritzker Prize acceptance speech. 'Together, these disciplines represent for me a fantastic platform for experimentation and expression.'

It is no wonder that Murcutt has become such a figurehead, despite his modesty and quiet approach. In so many ways his houses sum up the key qualities of the new natural home at its best: flexibility, sensitivity, contextuality, longevity and beauty, all delivered with the lightest of touches. These are homes of authentic originality that avoid gimmicks, fashion and fads.

New Natural Living

There was a point in the early days of the green revolution when there was something of a rush towards technology, gadgets and high-tech solutions that would instantly offer a way to green our homes. Many of these gadgets – for instance, wind turbines stuck onto the roofs of suburban homes – were little more than expensive gestures with little or no long-term benefit.

This book takes a very different approach in seeking to inspire change by presenting a wide range of houses from across the world – in many different contexts and situations – that are based in a more practical attitude to sustainability. They address essential themes such as solar gain, insulation, ventilation and material choices before moving on to issues such as home energy production. In other words, the necessity of conserving and managing energy – while establishing a successful working relationship with the natural world – lies at the heart of the new natural home and must come before, or in concert with, the generation of renewable energy.

These are inspirational, aspirational and thoughtful homes, as well as being sustainable. They are not about making do with something 'alternative' or unalluring. They are simply better houses in every way, as well as forming the enticing home front of the green revolution.

They are not about making do with something 'alternative' or unalluring. They are simply better houses in every way, as well as forming the enticing home front of the green revolution.

Opposite and above Glenn Murcutt's Simpson-Lee House in rural Mount Wilson, NSW, Australia, fits perfectly with his philosophy of touching the earth lightly. The house respects, preserves and celebrates the surrounding woodland while opening itself up to the natural world. Water-storage pools enhance the relationship between house and nature while also providing a valuable resource in case of forest fires.

1 | design & build

design & build

Second Nature

Over the coming decades, what may seem like pioneering architecture to us now will gradually become second nature. The rich and varied elements of the new natural home will become accessible and familiar, and the idea of sustainability will have established itself as an intrinsic part of our approach to the design and build of our homes.

Yet the challenge of creating beautiful, individual and enduring living spaces will remain, as the choices involved in designing and constructing an ecologically responsible house continue to be complex and often daunting. There is, after all, no underestimating the amount of personal commitment and creative energy needed to create a bespoke living space tailored to individual needs. But there should be no question of the many day-to-day benefits of enjoying a home that is not only green but also fits around the way you and your family want to live.

As we emerge from an era of consumer excess and reckless waste, we continue to demand beauty, originality and presence from architecture – particularly our homes – as well as a common-sense approach to sustainability. The green agenda may thread through the new natural home, but our focus also remains on creating enticing spaces that are welcoming, comfortable and endearing, as well as reflecting – in one way or another – our own personalities and aesthetics.

The key to this shift towards a second-nature approach to integrating green design solutions is to see the idea of sustainability not as a drawback or burden, but simply as a positive and necessary theme to be woven into the fabric of our homes, one that can only improve it and make it more economical in the long term, as well as benefiting the environment. The green approach to inventing a new home can bring only advantages rather than compromises, but needs to be woven into the design process from the very start.

Eco-economics

As well as environmental concerns and the issue of developing a home that is both practical and beautiful, the other great incentive pushing forward the concept of the new natural home is financial. As the cost of energy to power and heat our homes continues to rise – and looks set to carry on doing so for the foreseeable future, even as renewable energy becomes increasingly important – the impetus to reduce the amount we spend on our energy bills becomes more and more obvious.

There are many steps that any homeowner can take to insulate their home better to save on bills for heating and cooling while also looking at generating their own energy in one form or another, such as ground-source heat pumps or biomass boilers (see Chapter 5). Building a home from scratch provides a unique opportunity to design not just an ergonomic and bespoke dwelling but also one that takes a considered approach to power and energy right from the start, with the aim of cutting down on energy use and bills in the long term.

Like all good design, this demands a great deal of careful thought and time within the design process itself. Above all, it requires an approach that seeks to work with the specific site, climate and surroundings rather than working against nature.

Clear Vision

The often intense but highly rewarding process of designing and building a home is one of collaboration. At the root of the well-designed home is a successful, even extraordinary, relationship between client and architect that can in many respects be very personal and long-lasting. While other consultants, engineers

Pages 16–17 Sixteen Doors, New York, by Adam Rolston of Incorporated Architecture & Design.

Opposite Rasmus Larsson of Design By Us and his wife Andrea, an interior stylist, created this family summer house in the Danish coastal town of Liseleje. The bespoke timber home includes a sheltered outdoor dining area and a wraparound deck reaching out into the grounds and woodland.

As we emerge from an era of consumer excess and reckless waste, we continue to demand beauty, originality and presence from architecture ... as well as a common-sense approach to sustainability.

Above A mesmerizing landscape view, as seen from a balcony window on the upper storey of the Portsea House, Australia, by Chris Connell Design.

Opposite Architect Ron Radziner designed his family home in Venice, CA, as a bespoke sanctuary, with a vibrant union between indoor and outdoor spaces. Principal living areas adjoin the surrounding gardens and terraces, as well as the swimming pool, which forms a fluid courtyard.

and surveyors will no doubt be involved along the way, it is this powerful and unique creative relationship – which could be compared to that between doctor and patient – that has to generate the momentum to carry a project forward.

While the process of selecting an architect usually relies on responses to his or her existing work or ideas, the best clients are those who come to a project with a good idea of what they want from a house and how they will live in and use their building. To begin with, this may simply be a folder of magazine cuttings or the ticketed pages of architecture and interiors books, or it might be a more sophisticated and accomplished brief.

The point is that no architect likes to be given carte blanche, and no designer wants to work in a vacuum or without a clear understanding of the needs of the end user. The house has to be the most intricate and complex product you will ever use, and arguably the most important, but a truly successful design will evolve only from a long process of discussion and consultation that gets to the very heart not just of personal taste but also of detailed requirements for day-to-day living.

There is, in other words, a sense of responsibility that comes with being a good client as well as a commissioned architect. It is a responsibility to get intimately involved in the design process from the start and to work hard to convey likes and dislikes, priorities and concerns.

One starting point could be that pile of books and magazine cuttings; another might be touring existing architect-designed houses and talking through ideas that work and others that don't in the hope of promoting a creative dialogue. Another good starting point is a look at your existing home – even if it's a temporary rental – to ask yourself what you like and dislike about it and how you would assess its benefits and shortcomings. Only through such creative dialogue can a tailored, practical, hard-working and desirable home begin to evolve.

The Flexible House

It should also be remembered that a truly sustainable home is one that is flexible. The house that survives and flourishes over centuries is one that can easily adapt and change according to the shifting needs, priorities and lifestyles of its owners.

To some extent this involves projecting ahead and looking at how the layout and design of the house can be made as malleable as possible. This is not just a question of planning in extra bedrooms, but also a more complex balancing act looking at, for instance, the provision of open-plan living spaces as well as more private retreats and escapes. It may involve creating multi-purpose rooms which can easily be adapted to different uses, such as playrooms or studies.

In the longer term, the flexible home should also be open to more dramatic change, with the possibility to extend, update or reinvent certain parts. Again, this is something to bear in mind both in positioning and designing a new building. Period barns, city warehouses and farmsteads have proven themselves wonderfully flexible and able to change, becoming contemporary family homes and lofts, for example. This is the kind of flexibility that gives long life and character to a building that is the opposite of short shelf-life housing stock.

'Houses become assets and as such pass through generations,' says British architect John Pardey. 'So the more permanent they can be in terms of catering for varying lifestyles and in their choice of materials, then overall the more enduring their future and this is real sustainability. Things like heating systems may come and go, but

the fabric should provide a stable platform in form and function for generations.'

Site Specifics

While any new house is the result of a particular, and ideally detailed, brief, the new natural home should also be a response to a specific site. Different sites – from urban to rural and everything in between – will demand very different responses, in part following on from concerns about neighbouring buildings, privacy, services and infrastructure. But the design of a home should also take great account of the geography and conditions of a site, seeking to use them to best advantage.

At its most poetic, this may involve the framing of the landscape and particular views from parts of the building – while also ensuring privacy – as well as maximizing the flow of natural light according to the seasonal track of the sun (see Chapter 2). But it also will take into account the topography of a site, seeking to work with the existing shape of the landscape as far as possible, rather than simply imposing a building on the land.

This is, of course, a very different approach from, for example, the grand Neoclassical country house, which generally sought to dominate the landscape while creating an artificial and complementary landscape of parkland as well as formal gardens. Today, the approach tends to be very different, with architects – and landscape designers – increasingly seeking to work with an existing landscape and veering towards more naturalistic planting, while preserving as much of the original tree and plant life as possible.

Architect Barrie Marshall, of Denton Corker Marshall, took the idea of a sensitive approach to landscape to an extreme with his own home at Phillip Island, Australia (see page 230). Marshall was so concerned about limiting the effect of his holiday house on a coastal landscape of outstanding beauty that he largely buried it within the rugged dune and scrub terrain. The house, then, mostly disappears into the shoreland, making only the slightest of tectonic marks.

Many of the projects in this book feature houses that have also been partly shaped by their site and the landscape, rather than seeking to level off a building plot and start from scratch. It is partly a common-sense outlook which aims to preserve the beauty or unique characteristics of a site and enhance those qualities that may have drawn you to that particular spot in the first place.

Music of Time

As part of a contextual response to a specific site, time is an invaluable resource. It takes time to understand how the daily and seasonal pattern of shifting sunlight might affect a building, as well as to learn which aspects or vistas might best be taken advantage of by sightlines from within the new building.

Glenn Murcutt talks of truly understanding a site before putting pen to paper, including the way it might be exposed to a specific local climate, and how a house might settle into the topography accordingly. 'I'd been going up there for a year and a half before starting work on the house and understood the weather patterns and the rain and the wind,' he has said of the Marie Short House (see page 102), now his own country home. 'They were very important things to be aware of. It was my first country house and released within me ideas that I'd been working with for a long time.'

In the UK, Steve and Dee Hind bought a small bungalow on a beautiful site by the River Loddon – a tributary of the Thames – with the aim of building a contemporary replacement house to be designed by John Pardey (see page 34). They spent two years living in the existing house before starting work on the new build, getting to know and understand the location and the area and what they really wanted from the new house, as well as making friends with their neighbours.

This slow and careful approach allows for a depth of understanding that inevitably feeds into and affects the quality and thoughtfulness of the finished home. It is a quality entirely missing from many rapid-fire housing developments, so often more about maximizing volume and revenue rather than the kind of view residents might have out their windows, or an understanding of ways to make the most of natural light or respond to local extremes in weather and climate.

High-spec Investments

Time and preparation spent drawing up a detailed brief and wish list, based on a real understanding of the site, will not only deliver a better home but should also help in preparing an exact budget. Using more in the way of local materials and labour should help reduce costs and transportation miles, but it is important to bear in mind that investment up front in key aspects of a new natural home will be vital in keeping a cap on future running costs and managing energy use.

Some of these elements do not sound particularly glamorous and will be more or less invisible, but are key to the sustainable home. While there may be many questions around the subject of materials (see Chapter 3), certain choices may partly be dictated

Opposite Adam Rolston, of Incorporated Architecture & Design, designed a weekend house for himself and his partner in upstate New York in a tranquil rural setting. With open-plan living spaces within, and the use of many natural materials, this sustainable home reaches out to the surrounding landscape through large banks of glazing to either side.

by the need to conserve energy in the long term and keep the building at a constant temperature. Despite the high embodied energy and CO_2 emissions involved in making concrete, for instance – which make it a rather questionable eco-material – it is still generally used for foundations and floor pads, as it is not only a powerful structural material but also has a high thermal mass. This helps keep a building at a more regulated temperature than some lighter-weight choices.

Other eco-friendly ideas such as rainwater harvesting are best to consider early on, as retrofitting rainwater-collecting tanks can be very difficult, given the earthworks involved in installing large underground chambers. These – along with greywater recycling – make a huge amount of sense in areas of low and limited rainfall. In areas of higher rainfall such as Northern Europe, their benefits may never really outweigh the investment needed in installation costs.

Above all, there is the question of insulation, which has to be of very high specification for walls, floors and ceilings to help in retaining heat in cool climates and in keeping a house cool in warmer conditions.

Insulation by Design

Simply put, there is always going to be limited benefit to any other eco-measures – such as home-energy micro-generation – if a house is poorly insulated. It is one of those few subjects in home design that is not contentious and can be retrofitted to existing houses as well as integrated into new builds and extensions. Given that such a high proportion of home power use is devoted to heating and cooling, insulation has to be a priority.

In recent years, natural materials such as sheep's wool and hemp – as well as fibreboard – have become increasingly popular choices for insulation, not just because they are intrinsically green but also because they have a high performance value that can outstrip other synthetic alternatives. Natural insulation materials, which also include cellulose from recycled paper and flax, are becoming increasingly available and are taking a greater share of the market.

But any insulation choice has to be better than none – there are also an increasing number of insulation materials using recycled materials – given that poor insulation and poor detailing will create a self-defeating home. For those on tighter budgets, then, a pragmatic choice of the lowest-cost insulation, even synthetic versions, is understandable.

PassivHaus and Ventilation

High-spec insulation is a key component of the PassivHaus concept, which originated in Germany and has been gaining more and more international attention. Particular emphasis is placed on super-insulating the home and ensuring that there are no thermal gaps that could lead to energy loss. Windows are triple-glazed and the house must meet a rigorous standard of air tightness. Such houses use mechanical ventilation to circulate fresh air with a heat-recovery system for colder climates that recaptures around 75 per cent of heat as stale air is exhausted from the house. The PassivHaus concept aims to vastly reduce the need for heating or cooling in the first place, keeping the building at a constant temperature and avoiding the need to expend large amounts of power generating heat or running air-conditioning systems.

Many new natural homes integrate a more flexible approach and rely on nature to deal with the question of ventilation rather than on mechanical ventilation systems. While integrating high-performance insulation as standard, these eco-houses use natural cross breezes from opening windows and doorways, as well as including ventilation slits that can be easily sealed and unsealed. Opening skylights at the top of a house will also help to draw out hot air naturally, replacing it with cool air drawn in from windows or ventilation gaps at ground-floor level.

The idea of circulating air is vital, not just to naturally cooling a home, but to the sense of well-being that comes from constantly or regularly introducing fresh air. When a building becomes totally sealed, problems begin with sick-building-type symptoms.

Again, this is a return to the themes of working with nature rather than against it, and of common sense. Simply opening the windows on a summer's day to get a fresh breeze makes us feel better and healthier than any air-conditioning unit. But at the same time we want to be draught-free and able to conserve and retain heat during a chill night. The sustainable home, then, is a flexible home in more senses than one.

SUMMARY

General

* Time spent in forward planning and creating a detailed brief for a home build will pay off in the quality of the house and its ability to save on energy bills in the long term.
* Look at examples of houses you admire for inspiration and ideas. Borrow ideas and principles from past and present architecture.
* Draw up files of cuttings from magazines and newspapers that may help both in developing a brief for your home and establishing a strong dialogue with your architect.
* Remember that the architect–client relationship is a very personal one that carries over a considerable period of time. Ensure that you get on with your architect, as well as admiring his or her work.
* Provide dialogue and guidance to enable your architect to progress. Commissioning any building, conversion or extension carries a responsibility to be clear about the direction in which you want to go and what you expect from the finished results.
* Draw on the expertise of other consultants and specialists, especially surveyors and 'eco-auditors' who can provide detailed advice on energy-saving approaches.
* Be prepared to keep a close eye not just on the evolution of the designs but also on the build itself. Even if you have an expert project manager, be prepared to step in if you are unhappy with the progress or direction of your project.

Forward Thinking

* Plan any major ground works or site upheaval as early as possible. These might include rainwater-harvesting storage tanks, wells and coiled pipes or boreholes for a ground-source heat pump – works that would be disruptive to retrofit.
* Build in a degree of flexibility to the design of the house that will allow the structure to evolve according to changes in lifestyle and/or family requirements.
* Consider the balance between open-plan living areas and more intimate, private retreats, while including some spaces that could easily be adapted to different uses.
* From the start, try to think of ways in which the house could be extended or enlarged in future and try to plan accordingly by, for instance, routing services via areas that are unlikely to be disturbed for enlargement.
* Skimping and saving on key elements such as insulation and structural integrity could compromise the long-term performance of the building and lead to lost energy and higher running costs. Creating a high-performance thermal shell is an essential investment.

Site Specifics

* Take time, along with your architect, to get to know your site, including its relationship to the landscape as well as weather patterns and the way the sun will work its way around your future home.
* Be contextual in creating something that tries to work with the landscape and topography, rather than levelling the site and imposing an alien object upon it.
* Respect existing planting, landscaping and woodland where possible. Be prepared to plant or replant trees and shrubs when the build is over.
* Carefully consider the way the house will be positioned on the site, not just in terms of taking the best advantage of natural light but also to frame particular vistas and points of interest.
* Look at ways to mitigate the impact of the house on the landscape by considering not only natural and local materials but also ideas such as green roofs and even submerging or pushing parts of the house into the topography.
* Respect the privacy of neighbours – as well as your own – and look at ways to reduce any intrusion or overlooking.

Insulation

* Insulate, insulate, insulate. Make insulation of walls, roof and floors – along with low-emissivity glazing – a priority in any new build, extension or home-improvement plan.
* Consider natural insulation materials not only for their wider ecological friendliness but also because they perform better than many synthetic alternatives.
* Good alternatives to natural insulation include some types of recycled materials and fibres, among them insulation made out of recycled plastics and glass.
* Never skimp on insulation costs to save money up front as this will be a false economy and threaten the future energy efficiency of your home.

Ventilation

* If you are going for a PassivHaus approach with super-insulation and super air tightness, ensure that you install a mechanical ventilation and heat-recovery system to maintain the circulation of fresh air.
* Mechanical ventilation with heat recovery can be used in any home to expel stale air while 'recycling' warm air back into the house.
* Consider natural cross-ventilation ideas and a natural 'exhaust' system that draws in cool air from the lower levels and expels hot air from operable skylights at the top of the building.
* Install flexible louvres or ventilation gaps which can be opened on hotter days but easily and efficiently sealed during colder spells.
* Consider dehumidifiers as well as natural ventilation options if there is a considerable danger of excess humidity building up in the home, which can lead to poor air quality as well as problems with dampness and mildew.

'The house really uses low-cost ideas in a pleasingly simple way, with a strong emphasis on unadorned quality materials.'

DANGAR HOUSE, DANGAR ISLAND, NSW, AUSTRALIA

ROBERTSON & HINDMARSH ARCHITECTS

Situated on a small island in the mouth of the Hawkesbury River, north of Sydney, the Dangar House took some time to evolve. Given its location at the heart of an area of outstanding beauty, with a number of nature reserves close by, the planning process was slow and drawn out, involving a series of careful surveys to look at any potential impact of the building on the local environment and plant life. The benefit of this three-year planning process was that by the time construction finally began, homeowners David Harrison and Karen McCartney had ironed out exactly what they wanted from the house and its design.

Based in Sydney, Harrison and McCartney were looking for a weekend escape for themselves and their two children. They found some land on Dangar Island that already had a poorly built shack on it and – working with architects Robertson & Hindmarsh – developed designs for a new cabin on the rugged, sloping site. The new building is raised up on steel supports to create an even platform that provides a strong, elevated viewing deck above the fauna and on a level with the lower sections of the surrounding tree canopy. 'The brief was to create a very open space that captured the views and as much northern light as possible,' says architect Jan Robertson.

During the drawn-out planning process, Harrison – a writer and stylist – and McCartney – a magazine editor – debated whether or not to include guest accommodation. Thinking ahead, they decided to bite the bullet and include a guest wing positioned at a slightly lower level to the main house, with its own private terrace and stairway access to the grounds and a private beach nearby. 'It was a couple of extra months of building time but only a small additional cost so it was pretty enticing. The idea was to allow guests to have the autonomy to come and go as they pleased,' says Harrison.

This arrangement created a level of flexibility within the design of the three-bedroom home, while the open space under the northern section of the house has been earmarked as an area in which to create an additional work space or studio in the future.

The house was built by local builders, with all materials brought to the island by barge and boat. There is a pleasing balance between indoor and outdoor space and a fluid relationship between the two. The dominant material is timber, with Australian blackbutt cladding, merbau for window frames, local stringybark for the decks and internal floors in American oak.

Only three small trees were cut down during the build, and the cabin sits lightly on its supporting pillars, respecting the integrity of the site. The house includes rainwater harvesting for flushing the toilets, along with a natural filtration system for dealing with effluent. The underside of the building is coated in a fire-retardant layer of compressed cement, which also serves as additional insulation.

'It is a very calm and unpretentious house,' says Harrison. 'We like the simple palette of materials and finishes; Karen was inspired by a shot of a Scandinavian cabin stained grey. The house really uses low-cost ideas in a pleasingly simple way, with a strong emphasis on unadorned quality materials.'

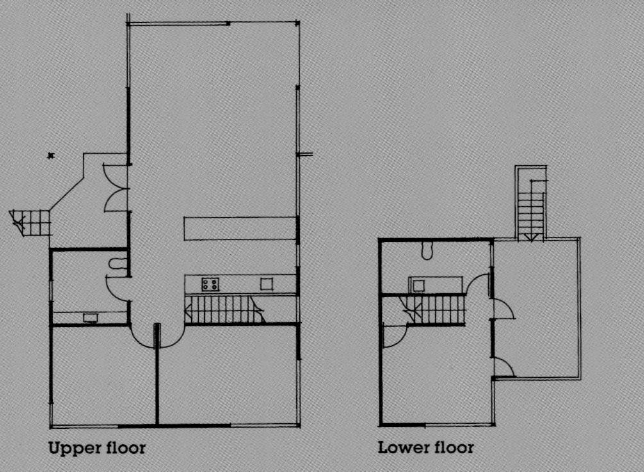

Pages 26–29 Perched on steel legs, the cabin has something of the feel of a tree house sitting almost within the green canopy of the surrounding woodland. Only three trees were felled to build the house, and the design accommodates and celebrates its surroundings.

Opposite and this page Easily accessed from the main living spaces, a deck creates an outdoor area for dining, relaxing and admiring the landscape. The guest annexe, at a slightly lower level, has its own terrace. Inside the house, large banks of floor-to-ceiling glazing – including glass doors opening on to the deck – bring in the rich natural light and offer a degree of transparency.

This page and opposite
Within the house, the palette of materials and colours is warm but simple, with a Scandinavian-inspired elegance. Natural materials dominate. 'Most of the furniture is in oak or teak, because I love those two timbers,' says David Harrison. 'The pieces in the house are a very personal collection of stuff acquired from friends who are artists, photographers and furniture makers along with other things that we have fallen in love with. Usually, anything destined for the Dangar House has to have a little bit of the handmade or the understated about it to work.'

The idea of a 'floating house' not only made it flood-proof ... but allowed the Hinds to benefit from the elevated vantage point, with the open-plan kitchen and dining and living area taking full advantage of the vista of the river.

HIND HOUSE, WARGRAVE, BERKSHIRE, UK

JOHN PARDEY ARCHITECTS

By the time Steve and Dee Hind asked John Pardey to design a house by the banks of the River Loddon in Berkshire, the architect already knew the area intimately. Some years earlier, he had worked on the reinvention of a 1960s home just along the access track that threads its way around this quiet and seductive area of natural beauty.

The Hinds bought a poorly built riverside bungalow here with the aim of replacing it with a contemporary home. But first they spent two years living in the existing house as they got to know their site and exactly what they wanted from their new building.

So the design of the Hind House was born from a mutual understanding of the particular delights and challenges of the location. While the house obviously needed to respond to the river and the landscape, it also had to take into account a very real risk of flooding, given that the river periodically breaks its banks in the winter months.

Pardey raised the house up on stilts to avoid flood risk and make the most of the views, with the structure positioned parallel to the river. But its orientation took into account many other factors as well. The idea of a 'floating house' not only made it flood-proof – a requirement that has already been dramatically tested to great effect – but allowed the Hinds to benefit from the elevated vantage point, with the open-plan kitchen and dining and living area taking full advantage of the vista of the river.

Sliding glass doors open the living spaces up to balconies and raised terraces while allowing natural cross-ventilation, which is enhanced by flexible ventilation slots. The master bedroom and bathroom of the four-bedroom house are positioned on a modest upper level, with a sculpted bath within the bedroom itself facing out across the Loddon.

The external fabric was super-insulated, and the low-emissivity double glazing is also high spec. Exposing the underside of the main living areas within the elevated design meant that particular attention was paid to thermal performance throughout, using sheep's wool insulation plus rigid urethane insulation for the roof.

Working closely with project manager Clive Hicks, Steve Hind involved himself in every aspect of the build. For Pardey, the results were especially pleasing. 'My hope was that it would have something of a timeless quality, by which I mean that it avoids fashionable trends or styles and has qualities that will endure,' he says. 'I believe that if a building like this gets well used then it is inherently sustainable because it serves a purpose. If it can endure and look after itself without a rigorous maintenance regime and adapt through time and not waste energy, then it will be a responsible building.'

Lady Dee Dee

Lower floor

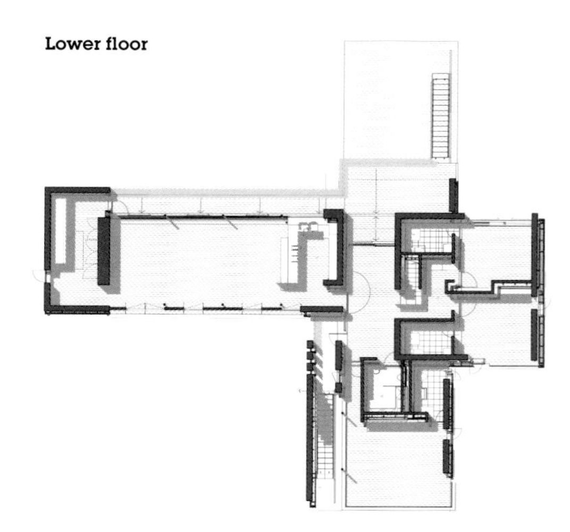

Upper floor

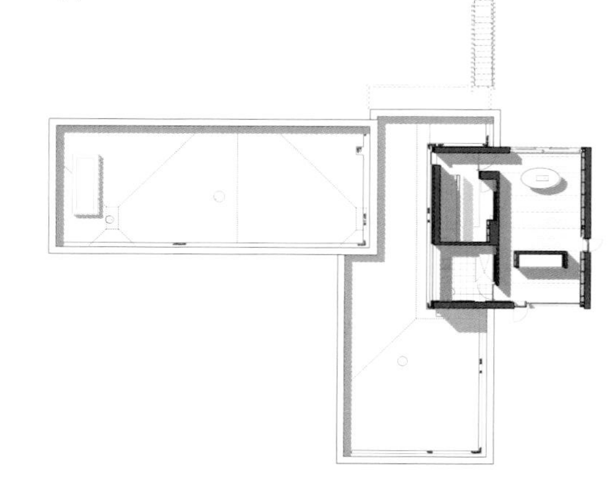

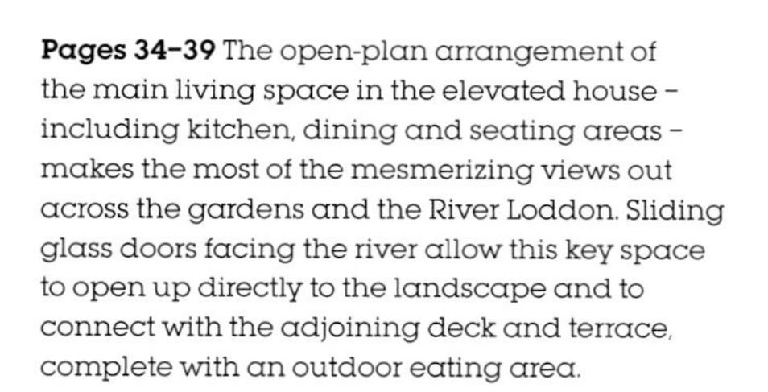

Pages 34–39 The open-plan arrangement of the main living space in the elevated house – including kitchen, dining and seating areas – makes the most of the mesmerizing views out across the gardens and the River Loddon. Sliding glass doors facing the river allow this key space to open up directly to the landscape and to connect with the adjoining deck and terrace, complete with an outdoor eating area.

Opposite and this page The elevated design of the building protects the house from flood risk while also allowing for appreciation of the landscape. The void underneath the house doubles as a carport. The master bedroom on the house's modest top level (above right) allows for views to both the front and the back.

'We only use air conditioning for perhaps two weeks of the year and only on the hottest days. The natural ventilation needs more involvement ... but it's so much nicer to have fresh air and not to be using energy.'

LOS FELIZ RESIDENCE, LOS ANGELES, CA, USA

TECHENTIN BUCKINGHAM ARCHITECTURE

Perched on a healthy slab of bedrock, Warren Techentin's Los Angeles home makes the most of its hillside location. Sitting within the leafy neighbourhood of Los Feliz, the house maximizes vistas of jacarandas and palms. For a city with limited green space and epic urban sprawl, this is a treat in itself, made all the better by the fact that Griffith Park is just around the corner.

But Techentin's home, shared with his wife Mimi Won Techentin and their two young children, was not always so desirable. The couple bought the site with a rather forlorn-looking 1950s bungalow sitting on top of a basement garage pushed into the slope of the hill. It has taken a radical rebuild to create a new, bespoke family home, enveloped in redwood cladding, stained and painted black, with a montage of distinctive green-framed windows enhancing views of the city.

'The foundations of the original house are still there, and some of the basement,' says Techentin, a principal of the Los Angeles architectural practice Techentin Buckingham. 'We were trying to save money on the build costs so the more we could do with the original foundation the better.'

The design of the house was partially dictated by the bungalow footprint, but is liberated by its two-storey layout, with key living spaces on the raised ground floor and bedrooms above, along with study space. Abundant storage and a high level of flexibility are woven into the design.

'As we are not on a wholly private site, we had to balance the need to open up the house with maintaining privacy,' says Techentin. 'Certain areas of the house like the open-plan sitting room and dining room – or "great room" – have large windows like landscape paintings that look out onto the neighbourhood. Other openings – especially to the side of the house – are more modest.'

The 'great room', with a window seat facing south towards the tree canopy, is the pivotal living space. A library to one side of the sitting room occupies the literal heart of the building, with the stairway wrapping around it as it ascends. The stairway doubles as a light well toplit by a skylight, while opening windows on the skylight turn the library into a natural ventilation stack.

'We only use air conditioning for perhaps two weeks of the year and only on the hottest days,' says Techentin. 'The natural ventilation needs more involvement – opening and closing the windows when you need to – but it's so much nicer to have fresh air and not to be using energy.'

Techentin is also installing solar panels on the roof, while insulation standards are high and glazing is low-emissivity with UV coatings. Some materials from the original house were recycled, while the redwood cladding (which coats a timber frame) was locally sourced from sustainable forestry, as well as being very hard-wearing.

'It's a great material in terms of resisting rot and bugs, which is why people use it so much here,' he says. 'There's a 3-inch gap between the cladding – which soaks up the heat – and the inner lining walls of the house, so that air flows between the two layers. The ventilation gap stops the heat from getting through to the inner walls and heating up the house. We have a very small footprint here, with tiny gas and power bills.'

Pages 42–45 Facing east, the kitchen derives its extraordinary luminescent quality from exterior walls coated in a translucent Polygel cellular plastic, most commonly used to make greenhouse walls. The coating creates an almost Japanese, lantern-like effect. The dining alcove – which leads into the main living room – was partly inspired by the booths of period American diners.

ALVAR AALTO
PREFAB PROTOTYPES
ARCHITECTURE STUDIO
SHIGERU BAN
BAUHAUS
Félix Candela
PIERRE CHAREAU
Affordable Housing
1000 chairs
CENTURY
All-American Ads
NEW YORK 1900
NEW YORK 1880
RE-WORKING EISENMAN
RALPH ERSKINE
FRANK
PARALLAX
THE LANDSCAPE OF MAN
A GENIUS FOR PLACE
The Western Garden Book
ARNE JACOBSEN
Le Corbusier
marcel duchamp
THE VILLAS OF LE CORBUSIER
KM3
MVRDV
FARMAX
WALLACE NEFF
MALEVICH
MOHOLY-NAGY
MOTHERWELL
NOX
RODCHENKO
PAUL RUDOLPH
KURT SCHWITTERS
SERRA
WORKERS
ROMAN SIGNER
THE SCIENCE OF ART
FROM ABOVE
MOTHER'S HOUSE
HOME DELIVERY
Michelangelo
False Flat
Topologies
SPACED OUT

Opposite and this page
The staircase wraps around the library, which sits at the heart of the building. The stairwell has an opening skylight above it, drawing in light but also serving as a natural ventilation stack, sucking hot and stale air from the top of the building.

Above and opposite The 'great room' is an open-plan space cradling dining and seating areas, with the library and timber stairway off to one side. The quality of light here is rich, with a large picture window and window seat facing south and positioned to take best advantage of the vista. The vibrant quality of natural light is also apparent in the master bedroom and bathroom, where even the shower area has its own window.

'What we can do, by opening up walls and so on, is to move the living space out of the house and into the landscape so that the house becomes a part of the entire property.'

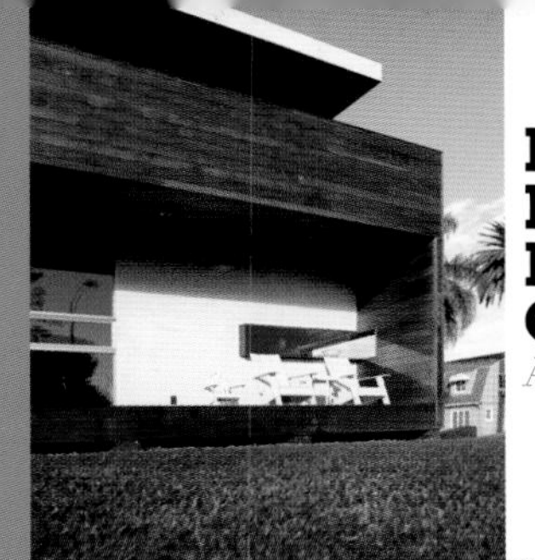

RIDGEWOOD HOUSE, LARCHMONT VILLAGE, LOS ANGELES, CA, USA

ASSEMBLEDGE+

The design of David and Jamie Thompson's Ridgewood House in Los Angeles presents a choice of outdoor rooms along with a fluid relationship between interior and exterior space. The house features a large front porch opening out to the lawned garden and the street. On the upper level of the house is a partly shaded roof terrace that offers a greater sense of privacy and some enclosure. To one side of the house, another substantial terrace sits on the roof of the partially sunken garage, while to the rear the family room is enhanced by a sliding glass wall opening up to the back garden.

Within this suburban context on a corner site, then, the house – shared with the Thompsons' two young children – forms a strong bond with its surroundings and a flexible connection between interiors and exteriors.

'One of the things that we try to do with all our residential projects is to look at the project in terms of the total square footage of the site, rather than just the square footage of the house,' says David Thompson, a principal at assembledge+. 'What we can do, by opening up walls and so on, is to move the living space out of the house and into the landscape so that the house becomes a part of the entire property rather than just a compartmentalized section of it. So we really use all of the site all of the time. The house is 2,400 square feet [223 square metres], but it feels as though it's much bigger than that because of all the useable space.'

Large banks of floor-to-ceiling glass in the living room to the front of the house, as well as the family room to the rear, reinforce the feeling of connection to the garden and offer some sense of transparency, contrasting with more closed elements of the building, which offer greater privacy. On the upper level, the master bedroom features sliding glass doors that open out onto the roof terrace, where the overhang of the flat roof offers some protection from the midday sun.

'The terrace by the bedroom is really wonderful,' Thompson says. 'With the building itself coming right up and forming this solid railing, it does feel very secluded. Once the sun gets higher in the sky it does get shaded by this big overhang and keeps cool. The doors open up from the bedroom and we generally sleep with them open every night.'

A semi-open-plan layout for the main living spaces on the ground floor helps natural light circulate, while the house benefits from natural cross-ventilation and also an operable skylight that helps vent hot air. The house is clad in red cedar from sustainable sources.

With its crafted approach and its emphasis on constant connections between indoor and outdoor living, this new California home sits very much in the tradition of the great pioneering West Coast Modernists such as Rudolph Schindler and Richard Neutra.

Pages 50–53 The house offers a great deal of choice between indoor and outdoor areas for relaxing and dining. The ground-level porch facing the street is complemented by the terrace on the upper level, which provides a stronger sense of intimacy and privacy while offering views out across the neighbourhood and the hills beyond. This emphasis on flexible living within a building that can adapt easily according to different programmes and needs is a hallmark of the new natural home.

Living spaces gently connect with outdoor zones and natural elements ... forming a close sense of communion with the environment and the changing seasons even in this suburban context.

WABI HOUSE, CARLSBAD, CA, USA

SEBASTIAN MARISCAL STUDIO

The unique design of the Wabi House was the result of a close collaboration between architect Sebastian Mariscal and his Japanese-born clients. The clients had been considering remodelling a 1970s home on their suburban site, but ultimately decided on a new-build project that would deliver a tailored, bespoke and more sustainable home.

'The clients were very important in the whole design process and it was a great collaboration,' says Mariscal. 'They were very organized and gave us a lot of feedback. We met many times to talk about their goals and dreams for the house and they put together a document listing the things that they liked and disliked. They didn't want a McMansion or a showy big house. They wanted the opposite – something discreet and introspective. This was one of their main priorities and for me this kind of feedback was great, because it's the kind of discussion that I'm looking for from a really good client.'

The resulting new natural home is an enticing and welcoming fusion of architectural ideas, with a strong Japanese influence and the integration of some traditional aspects of Japanese living reinterpreted in a contemporary way.

From the exterior, the house is enigmatic and very different from any of its more familiar suburban neighbours. The low-slung building has been purposefully tucked into the site to enhance privacy but also to create a process of discovery. The house is entered via a doorway in a border fence of charred cedar wood. Beyond this, a pathway leads to a small bridge over a pool and then to the formal entrance to the house. Moving into the home itself, the entryway has been modelled on the idea of the Japanese *genkan* – a calming hallway with cabinetwork – where outdoor shoes can be removed and stored and indoor slippers chosen.

Within the house itself, a key element is the emphasis on flexibility. The ground floor is dominated by a large open-plan living area and kitchen, with banks of retractable glazing leading out to a gravel garden and rear outdoor space. Sliding screens allow a guest bedroom and a study to be read as part of this overall central space or to be easily separated off and transformed into more private and intimate zones.

The master bedroom is situated on a modest upper level which leads out to a planted roof garden. Here, as on the ground floor, living spaces gently connect with outdoor zones and natural elements such as planting and pools, forming a close sense of communion with the environment and the changing seasons even in this suburban context. The pools and cross-ventilation also help with natural cooling in the hotter months.

'I wanted to understand how the clients wanted to live in the house and it became clear that they wanted a peaceful and serene atmosphere,' Mariscal says. 'The water pools help with that enormously and – together with the *genkan* – become a filter between the interior and the outside world.'

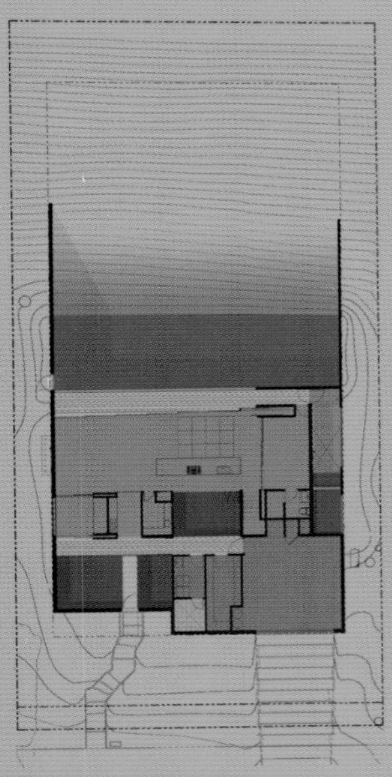

Ground floor

Upper floor

Pages 54–59 Approaching and entering the Wabi House offers a gradual process of discovery and revelation, as one passes through the enigmatic entrance, then across a bridge over water pools and finally into a Japanese-inspired *genkan*, or entrance hall, where outdoor shoes are stored and replaced by slippers. The house then unfolds and reveals itself as one passes into the main living room at the rear, where glass doors slide back to allow a smooth transition to the gravel garden.

Above and opposite The building's design incorporates an extraordinary degree of transparency, even within this suburban site, allowing the eye to pass through areas such as the open-plan kitchen/sitting room and into the gardens beyond. The house also allows for maximum flexibility, with sliding partitions permitting areas such as the study adjoining the sitting room to be read as part of one large, generous space (above left) or to be neatly separated for greater privacy.

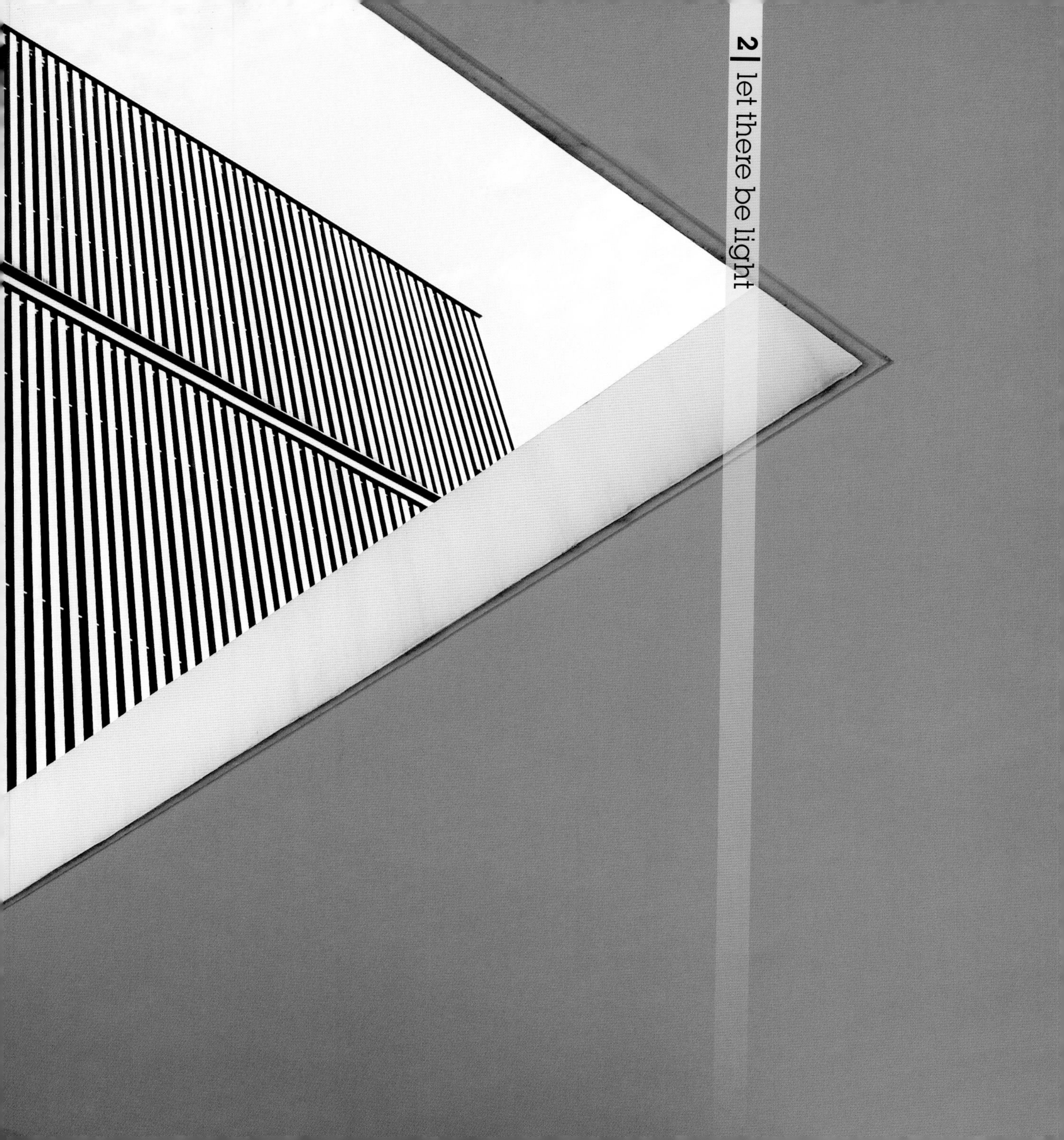

2 | let there be light

let there be light

The history of architecture is also the story of the creative manipulation of natural light. It is sunlight that truly brings spaces alive and allows the rich textures and character of a building and its materials to be appreciated. Good lighting represents the difference between a space that might seem oppressive and claustrophobic and one that is welcoming, bright and liberating.

Over the centuries the home, like so many other buildings, has been reinvented through the mastery of ideas and techniques that allowed light to permeate and invigorate interior space. One reason that Georgian architecture of both town and country proved so enticing was that it represented a shift away from low ceilings and small window openings and towards more generously proportioned rooms bathed in sunlight from large areas of glazing.

In the Victorian era, advancing industrial processes allowed for the mass production of glass while ambitious engineering made possible grand conservatories, botanic glasshouses and 'crystal palaces', as well as making glass more accessible and affordable for home use. Through the twentieth century, the revolution in home design was helped by new technology that allowed the manufacture of much larger and stronger panels of glass, thus enabling architects to work with natural light in startling and surprising ways.

This was coupled with the concept of the 'curtain wall', where the need for solid façades that helped support a building in materials like brick or stone was replaced with the use of supporting pillars or columns in iron, steel or concrete that freed up the face of a building so it could be infilled with glazing. In the late 1940s and early 1950s this in turn led to the idea of the transparent building and the invention of Philip Johnson's Glass House (1949) in New Canaan, Connecticut, and Mies van der Rohe's Farnsworth House (1951) in Plano, Illinois.

These highly influential and striking designs helped reshape attitudes to natural light, as well as to the design of the home itself. Johnson's Glass House is a completely glazed pavilion within a scenic private estate, with views out across woodland and a lake and valley below. The Glass House is essentially open in plan, with just one solid cylinder within containing a small shower room. The serenity of the house is maintained by sweeping away almost all service and utility aspects of a traditional home into a neighbouring building called the Brick House, which is as mysterious and closed as the Glass House is open and free.

The Farnsworth House seems to float above its rural site, supported on a series of small pillars, or piloti. Again, a steel frame allowed the entire single-storey, flat-roofed building to be glazed, so the house became transparent, open to a landscape that now seems to pass through it. Within, Mies adopted a semi-open-plan approach, using banks of cupboards and a central service core – complete with galley kitchen – that could allow spaces to be lightly divided without destroying the concept of a generous, fluid and almost uninterrupted multi-functional space. Opening out on to large complementary terraces, the house is bathed in natural light, with large sliding glass doors that blur even further the boundaries between inside and out. Some privacy is provided by tracked curtains, which can also help filter sunlight.

These two revolutionary Modernist houses – still strikingly beautiful and extraordinarily influential – took the idea of the transparent glass house to an extreme and suggested the degree to which the home could now be opened up to the landscape and to natural light. Other Modernist pioneers sought a more regular balance between open-plan living and private, intimate retreats within the home. But it was clear that there was now no reason not to invite sunlight into the house and take the best advantage of natural light in every possible way.

The Light House

Given that these experiments in light – by Johnson, Mies van der Rohe, Richard Neutra, Le Corbusier and others – happened several generations ago, one

The orientation of a house will have a huge impact on the quality of light filtering into it along with the amount of potential solar gain.

Pages 62–63 The Garlick Avenue House, Singapore, by Kerry Hill Architects.

Page 64 and above At Rasmus and Andrea Larsson's family summer house in Denmark, light floods into the interiors through large banks of glazing, while light materials and white painted floors help bounce light throughout the home.

Opposite Architect David Jameson designed the Jigsaw Residence in Bethesda, MD, for himself and his family, introducing a wealth of natural light sourced from many directions and in many different ways, including traditional glazing, sliding glass doors and clerestory windows.

might assume that the modern home would always be a welcoming, sunlit building. Yet, while there might now be few excuses for creating claustrophobic houses – even on compact sites – it is surprising how many poorly designed homes still suffer from a significant lack of natural light. This in turn means higher energy use, of course, as rooms are lit artificially to compensate. There is inevitably something rather soul-destroying about walking into spaces that need daytime artificial lighting, even at the height of summer, but it is still a common sight, even in many recently completed buildings.

The provision of natural light comes back to what architects will tell you are simply matters of common sense and essential aspects of the new natural home. It is a vital and key element to the design of any building and one that has to be taken into account right from the very beginning of the design process.

Positions of Trust

It would be hard to over-emphasize the importance of correctly positioning a house on its site, so as to form the best possible relationship with the movements of the sun, as well as the surrounding landscape. The orientation of a house will have a huge impact on the quality of light filtering into it along with the amount of potential solar gain – the level of natural heating provided through glazing by the sun.

Successful orientation is a site-specific task that takes time. Generally, homes in the northern hemisphere tend to be orientated southwards and those in the southern hemisphere orientated northwards so as to enjoy the best of the natural light. But within this broad generalization there are many provisos according to the nature of the climate and the kind of topography the house might sit within.

With some sites, access to natural light may be limited by the topography or tree canopy – or the need to address a particularly outstanding view – thus leading to a suitable orientation that also seeks to draw in any easily available sunlight. In colder climates, one might seek to maximize solar gain with a more direct relationship to the sun than in warmer climates, where greater attention might be paid to cooling down the house. In other words, once again, there is no one-size-fits-all solution but instead a need for a considered, thoughtful approach that best suits a particular set of needs and priorities. The aim is to deliver a quality of light that illuminates the building and its interior spaces in a way that enriches the character and quality of the home and makes it a more pleasurable and practical place to live in.

Tricks of the Light

Whatever the particular conditions and climate, there are many different ways of maximizing and improving the quality of natural light beyond the basic issue of orientation and aspect. Much depends, of course, on the general level of glazing woven into the design of the house itself.

Many building codes and regulations now demand a high standard of low-emissivity glass for any new homes or extensions – double- or triple-glazed – to ensure that the building's insulated envelope is not let down by poor-quality glass. Flexibility is also something to consider when specifying glass windows and doors and choosing options that allow not just easy access to outdoor spaces but the means to open up different parts of the house to create natural cross-ventilation when needed. Few of us may feel brave enough to opt for the level of transparency of the Farnsworth House or Johnson's Glass House, but many would opt for a more balanced approach that offers a suitable level of natural light, along with a

real sense of connection with outdoor terraces, verandas, gardens and landscape (see Chapter 4).

The creation of integrated outdoor spaces that push into the overall outline of the house – such as internal courtyards – can also have a big impact on the quality of natural light in the home. This can be seen to great effect in architect James Russell's design for his Brookes Street House in Brisbane, Australia, wrapped around an elevated central courtyard (see page 80), complete with grass lawn.

Beyond this, there are many other design tricks that can be used to improve the quality of natural light. Los Angeles-based architect John Friedman of John Friedman Alice Kimm Architects suggests that sourcing light from alternate directions in the same space will help to take best advantage of sunlight at different times of the day, as well as enhancing the light quality overall. 'We have a rule in the office that every room that we design should get light from at least two different orientations, preferably three,' says Friedman. 'We are always mixing different kinds of natural light which gives you a richer quality of light and makes the space more dynamic.'

Skylights are an often underutilized source of light and can be a huge asset in complementing standard windows and openings. As with the King Residence in Santa Monica (see page 96), Friedman suggests using roof lights butted up to internal walls painted white so the sunlight from above is bounced off the wall and into the room below.

Rooms and spaces with few other sources of natural light – such as stairwells – can be lifted dramatically by roof lights, becoming light wells that carry illumination deep into the heart of a house. The same principle lies behind the growing importance of sunpipes, which help 'transmit' or push natural light from openings in the roof down into internal spaces that would otherwise suffer from little or no sunlight.

Moving Light

The idea of carrying or transmitting natural light from space to space within the home is a very useful concept in the creation of inviting interiors that do not have to rely on artificial light. An open- or semi-open-plan layout – at least for prime living spaces – clearly helps light to travel through a house. In such areas – as in the Farnsworth House – zones for alternative uses can be lightly delineated without using solid walls. A change in floor level or wall covering can be enough to signal a shift in function or mood, while low-level storage cabinets that allow light to spill around them can be used as dividers or screens.

But even where more solid divisions are necessary to partition rooms, internal windows might be considered. These can also be a big help in parts of the house starved of natural light from conventional windows, such as corridors, landings or stairwells. Instead of solid doors, alternatives in translucent or frosted glass can be helpful, as can pocket doors that slide away when not in use. Glass, after all, does not need to be completely transparent to allow a useful degree of natural light to pass from space to space, and translucent alternatives can offer privacy without opting for an opaque solution.

The use of pale and reflective colours and surfaces can also help light to flourish, while darker materials and tones might better suit rooms more commonly used in the evenings, or smaller and more intimate spaces. Mirrors, too, can make an extraordinary difference to a room when used on a significant scale, helping to transform a dull space into a far more vibrant environment.

Shutters and Screens

While natural light makes a vast difference to the quality of interior space in the home, the sun can also play a part in overheating houses and creating glare that can be distracting and overbearing. The answer is usually to integrate shutters, screens or canopies that can mitigate any overbearing impact of the sun while still allowing the home to benefit from natural light.

Key to the provision of shading is the idea of flexibility. Shutters, for instance, are an old idea but highly practical and adaptable. Many Georgian and Victorian homes were designed with integrated internal shutters that could easily be closed off at night, adding an extra layer of insulation to the windows, or used to provide shade in the heat of the day. Many traditional homes in parts of Continental Europe and other regions of the world incorporated external shutters, which – again – offered additional insulation, shade and also protection from the elements, particularly when the house was not in use.

Shutters have been reinvented in the contemporary house, as can be seen, for instance, in the home of Marcell and Uli Strolz (see page 246) in Lech, Austria, where a series of external, heavy-duty sliding wooden shutters can be used to help protect the house from avalanche risk. These shutters can also be used at night or during the day to help reduce glare from the sun, which can be potentially overwhelming in the winter as the light is reflected off banks of snow.

Similarly, the holiday and weekend home in France that Vicky Thornton designed for herself (see page 238) can be partially closed up by a similar set of robust sliding wooden shutters fitted to the outside of the building. When the house is not in use, these shutters help provide additional

The idea of carrying or transmitting natural light from space to space within the home is a very useful concept in the creation of inviting interiors that do not have to rely on artificial light.

Page 68 Pivoting shutters, reclaimed from a hotel, offer choices for natural ventilation, light or shade at the home of architect Channa Daswatte in Kotte, Sri Lanka.

Above At Ron Radziner's home in Venice, CA, vast sliding glass doors lead out to semi-sheltered and shaded verandas and to the adjacent swimming pool. Here, a balance is struck between inviting light into the home and controlling and managing the high summer sun.

security and reduce the risk of storm damage to the windows.

The north-facing BR House in Brazil, designed by architect Marcio Kogan, is provided with a high degree of adaptability by a system of dramatic and retractable screens in local teak wood (see page 72). 'They act like an outer skin and have a natural super efficiency to adapt,' says Kogan, 'helping to control the flow of air and sunlight while retaining the warmth in the bedrooms at night.'

In such climates, the use of common-sense shading techniques – as well as natural cooling in the form of cross-ventilation from through-flow breezes – helps to reduce the need for energy-consuming air-conditioning machinery. Demand for air-conditioning units does seem to be falling in some parts of the world, as designers return to common-sense principles to cool their buildings, incorporating flexible ideas that help to shade and protect, as seen at the BR House.

Canopies are also used increasingly, carefully positioned at key points around the exterior. When placed high above large banks of windows, they can help to protect the home from solar gain at the hottest part of the day – when the sun is highest in the sky – while still allowing for a strong quality of natural interior light through the remaining hours of morning and afternoon. They may also double as sun shades for outdoor terraces. Increasingly, such canopies are being designed as sculpted objects in themselves, complementing the design of the house alongside.

Balancing the need for light and shade is not always an easy task, which takes us back to the need truly to understand and appreciate the particular conditions of a site and the way the sun will travel over and around a building, not only during the course of the day but through the changing seasons. Natural light is an essential need in the home, but a flexible method that offers some way to control excessive sunlight and solar gain – even if just at the height of summer – can also make a great difference to the experience of living in and enjoying the new natural home.

SUMMARY

General

* A high quality of natural light not only lifts the mood of the home but cuts down on energy used to light dark and underlit spaces.
* Take account of the need to introduce sunlight into the home when positioning a building or extension and throughout the design process.
* Generally, homes in the northern hemisphere tend to be orientated southwards and in the southern hemisphere northwards to make the most of available natural light.
* Be flexible, as many factors determine how a house will be positioned. Who would want to turn their back on a stunning ocean view just to make sure their house was facing in the best direction for the sun?
* There will still be lots of design tricks and ideas that can be brought into play to ensure that the house benefits from plenty of natural light, even if it's not possible to orientate it to take best advantage of the movement of the sun.
* Consider the issue of privacy when positioning glazing, not only your own but that of your neighbours. Frosted and translucent glass can offer an alternative to fully transparent glazing where privacy is an issue.
* When designing a new-build home or extension, look at creating internal courtyards or outdoor terraces that push into the outline of the building itself, as such spaces can be highly valuable in drawing sunlight deep into the home.
* Ensure that any new glazing is in low-emissivity glass where possible, double- or triple-glazed.
* Also make sure that any window frames or skylights are securely and properly fitted to avoid compromising the thermal envelope and insulation of the building.

Introducing Light

* Look for extensive glazing in parts of the house that are most commonly used during the day and where a sense of connection is needed with a terrace or a particularly strong vista.
* Flexibility is key when choosing windows and glazed door systems. Look for solutions that allow easy access to outdoor space, as well as providing the opportunity to make the most of natural cross-ventilation.
* Remember that open-plan layouts – especially in the main living areas – help natural light to travel through the home.
* Use stairwells, corridors and landings where possible as conduits for natural light rather than creating dark and gloomy spaces. Such spaces can be used as light wells to draw illumination into the heart of the home.
* Illumination sourced from different aspects and directions in the same room or space can help to enrich the quality of light and make the area seem more dynamic. Consider windows and openings facing in multiple directions to benefit most from the movement of the sun through the day.
* Skylights can be a huge help in enriching spaces, sourcing light directly from above and drawing it down into the home. When used in stairwells and other access areas, they can become valuable light wells.
* Consider access issues to glazing and skylights to ensure that they can be opened, closed and cleaned when necessary.
* Look carefully at the way in which skylights are positioned and whether they will help to introduce sunlight where it is most needed. Positioning skylights alongside internal walls painted in light and reflective colours is one way of successfully bouncing light into a room.
* Sunpipes – 'solar tubes' or 'sun scoops' – are becoming a positive alternative method of introducing light to areas that otherwise might be starved of natural illumination, such as basements or areas trapped at the centre of the floor plan.
* Light and reflective surfaces help transmit sunlight around rooms and open spaces. Darker materials and shades might best be suited to more intimate, evening spaces and smaller rooms.
* Mirrors can make a big difference to light quality, especially when used in combination with other features such as skylights.
* When using artificial lighting, avoid incandescent bulbs. Look for low-energy alternatives, notably compact fluorescents. Energy-efficient halogen bulbs and LEDs offer alternatives.

Shade and Screening

* While solar gain – natural warming from the sun – can be a big boost in warming homes in cooler climates and colder parts of the year, it's also important to consider the drawbacks of overheating in summer.
* Make sure that your glazing systems are flexible so that windows, doors and skylights can be easily opened and closed to make the most of cross-ventilation and the natural venting of hot air through operable skylights, while drawing in cool air at lower levels.
* Flexible shutters and screens can be a huge benefit in providing shade when it is most needed. They are also good additional insulators and – when fitted externally – can help to protect the building from the elements, especially when it is not in use.
* Blinds and curtains of all kinds can also be used to provide shade and privacy. Operable blinds should be integrated into skylights where there is a risk of overheating or in spaces such as bedrooms where blackout may be needed in the summer months.
* Canopies at high level over banks of glazing can help to filter the effects of the sun at the peak of the day. Such canopies can double as awnings to protect terraces positioned alongside the house.
* Consider white, light or reflective surfaces – including insulating paints – for canopies and roof finishes, to help reflect sunlight and prevent heat build-up in warmer climates.
* Overhanging or projecting eaves and roof lines can help to protect more vulnerable parts of a building from direct sun.
* Louvred shutters assist in offering shade when needed but also allow the through-flow of fresh air. Combinations of sliding glazing and sliding louvred shutters can offer a highly flexible system that allows for light, shading, cooling and insulation in different variations.

Nature ... seems to push into the house itself with bedrock appearing to rise up from the floor around the pool and tree trunks emerging from slots in the elevated terrace.

BR HOUSE, PETRÓPOLIS, RIO DE JANEIRO, BRAZIL

MARCIO KOGAN

The BR House makes the most of its relationship to an extraordinarily vibrant and striking landscape. Situated within a verdant valley, bordered by rainforest, near the town of Petrópolis – around one and a half hours' drive north of Rio de Janeiro – the new house for private clients benefits from vast panoramic windows that not only draw in the light but also frame seductive views of the greenery.

But this is also a highly flexible home, facing north, with a second skin of sliding screens surrounding the upper level and made of cumaru, a local teak hardwood. These screens, offering a fresh protective layer beyond the glazing, can be used to provide shade and additional insulation, as well as added protection for the building itself. This is an area of warmth and humidity plus high rainfall, but in the winter the temperature can fall dramatically. The double layering of glass and timber screens offers an effective way to deal with these potential extremes while also allowing for natural cross-ventilation.

'The house was established in a delicate manner, where the upper floor that houses the living area and bedrooms has a good deal of glass, creating a super-strong relationship with nature,' says Kogan. 'At night the house illuminates like an enormous lantern in the midst of all the trees.'

The two-storey steel-framed house is accessed at the upper level via a long steel-and-timber walkway, which reaches indoors from a parking area some distance away. The bridge reinforces the idea of the house as a kind of floating viewing platform, or belvedere, sitting on a series of piloti, with the main living spaces on the upper floor enjoying this unique elevated vantage point. The kitchen acts as a buffer zone between the large, open living room and the four bedrooms. The ensuite bathrooms are mostly situated at the centre of the house – with the exception of the master bath – and all benefit from roof lights.

A large elevated deck or solarium is situated to the rear of the house, near the bridge entry area, with steps leading down to ground level and a more modest, discreet lower storey. Here, a swimming pool is protected by a wall of sliding glass, which retracts to form an instantly open relationship with the natural surroundings. Sauna, bathroom and service areas sit alongside the pool, all contained within a neatly recessed block, partly faced with local stone, surrounded by a partially shaded terrace, protected by the overhang of the living level above.

The use of local stone and timber helps to reinforce the connections back to nature, which seems to push into the house itself with bedrock appearing to rise up from the floor around the pool and tree trunks emerging from slots in the elevated terrace. The house, then, gives the impression of fitting in with the natural conditions of the site – and appreciating them – rather than imposing itself on the land.

'Passing over the bridge to the house,' Kogan says, 'you walk among this spectacular scenery: the forest, with its incredible variety of birds, flowers of every colour imaginable, the trees and the scent of the vegetation, as well as a small river and its marvellous sound. It is truly fantastic.'

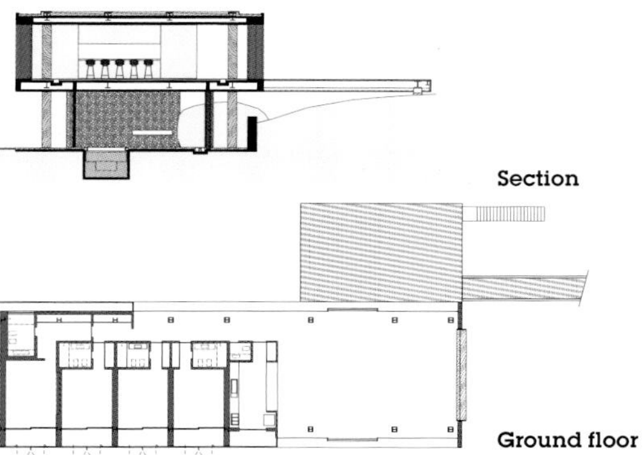

Pages 72–75 A vast window in the living room of this elevated home offers a view of the entrance bridge that forms part of the dramatic approach to the building. In some respects, the house becomes a balancing act between ideas of transparency and mass, while also serving as a belvedere, offering views of the lush jungle in all directions.

Opposite and above The design of the building and its approach to the control and manipulation of natural light are highly flexible. Folding latticed shutters made of a local hardwood create a protective skin that offers shade and shelter from the elements, while also playing a valuable role in helping to cool the house when needed. When closed, the shutters still allow a seductive, diffused light to permeate the interiors.

This page and opposite
With the main living spaces on the upper level offering a powerful viewing platform and a real sense of connection with the surrounding treescape, the protected lower level is free for other uses. Here Kogan has designed a semi-sheltered swimming pool with – again – a high degree of flexibility that allows the pool area to be opened up to the landscape and nearby sun terrace or closed down and protected when not in use. A solarium at the rear of the house, on the upper level, offers an alternative deck area.

'Beautiful light comes into the courtyard and deep into the rooms around it through a sawtooth roof ... and shade screens can be dropped down to help cool the house.'

BROOKES STREET HOUSE, BRISBANE, QLD, AUSTRALIA

JAMES RUSSELL ARCHITECT

One of the greatest challenges in the design of James Russell's home on a tight suburban site in Brisbane was the introduction of natural light. The architect acquired a nineteenth-century church building in the Fortitude Valley district of the city which was eventually converted into a furniture showroom. Russell then added an office for his practice and a pavilion housing a café, as well as a family home, which was positioned on a modest parcel of land between the church itself and a neighbouring period building.

'Introducing light and direct winter sun to the house was essential,' says Russell, who shares the building with his wife and three children. 'The outlook is south, south-west over Brookes Street, but the house is set back on the site, allowing the former church to be dominant on the street and screen us from the intense afternoon sun.'

The solid brick walls of the church itself form one side of the house, which is a tall and narrow three-storey building. The lower level forms a small commercial space – currently used as a studio and workshop – with an integrated staircase leading up and into the main body of the house, which opens out on the two upper levels. Here, a dramatic bank of double-height glazing faces Brookes Street, drawing in the available light.

The heart of the home is an elevated internal courtyard at the middle storey, complete with a small lawn, surrounded by the principal living spaces. This courtyard acts as an effective light well, while also providing secure, integrated outdoor space for the family, with a seamless transition between outside and in via sliding glass walls that can be pushed completely out of view.

'Beautiful light comes into the courtyard and deep into the rooms around it through a sawtooth roof,' says Russell. 'Midsummer sun is cut out by the roof as the sun moves overhead, and shade screens can be dropped down to help cool the house if the mid-season sun becomes too strong.'

Principal living spaces around the courtyard are largely open-plan, allowing light to pass through the lounge, kitchen/dining area, courtyard and family room as they benefit from a significant degree of transparency. Bedrooms are suspended within mezzanine structures on the upper level, connected by a floating bridge, all overlooking the central courtyard below. Additional light is drawn in at the top of the house via large roof lights.

A high level of flexibility is woven into the design, from the sliding glass walls around the courtyard to the built-in sun screens, plus louvred blinds in the family room, which offer privacy and additional shading. In this subtropical region the house relies on natural ventilation and has no air conditioning, easily adapting to changing weather patterns. The main materials are timber, steel, glass and concrete, which forms the structural core and which was chosen partly for its high thermal mass. Australian ironwood, ironbark and spotted gum timber were selected for durability and from sound sources and salvage. The house also benefits from solar panels, water recycling and storm-water storage tanks.

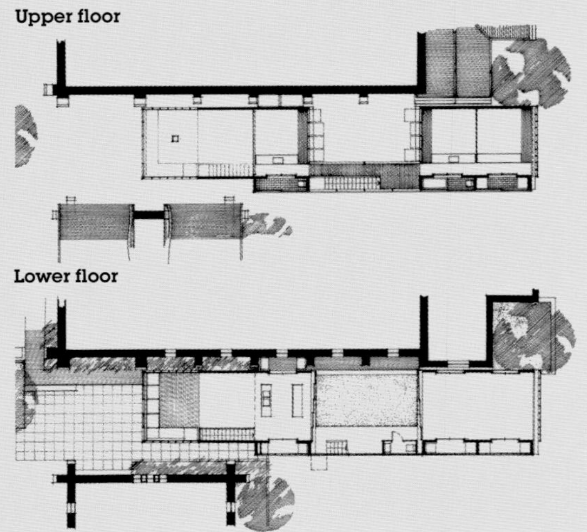

Pages 80–83 The house was designed around an elevated courtyard sky garden (complete with lawn), which acts as its hub and helps natural light to percolate deep into the principal living spaces. At the same time this integrated outdoor space is key to the family's day-to-day quality of life. 'The garden in the middle of our house offers an escape,' says Russell.

Opposite and above Sliding glass walls, screens, shutters and louvres combine to create a highly flexible system of light control, as well as a natural ventilation system. The creative manipulation of sunlight becomes part of the defining character of the home.

Above Bedrooms and bathrooms on the upper level look down into the garden court below, while shutter systems can be used to close down or open up these spaces.

Above Light is enticed into the house from large banks of glazing on the lower level and skylights on the top storey, but always in a controlled and defined manner.

'The central atrium ... helped create a sense of generosity in a very small house.'

HAUS W HAMBURG, GERMANY

KRAUS SCHÖNBERG ARCHITECTS

Surrounded by trees, Haus W sits on a generous green parcel of land on the outskirts of Hamburg. The planting offers a natural screen that allows privacy and encourages an architecture of openness, with the house connecting to the surrounding landscape and drawing in sunlight from all directions.

Due to planning restrictions, most houses in the area are only one storey, usually with a traditional pitched roof. But Henning and Ana Wachsmuth and their architects – the Anglo-German practice Kraus Schönberg – wanted to build a two-storey house, if on a modest scale.

'We knew that if we went to a certain point below ground level, then the lower floor would count as a basement,' says Timm Schönberg, who had known Henning Wachsmuth for many years, having studied architecture alongside him. 'So it became a simple trick to push the house into the ground and to achieve two full storeys that way. Then what really interested us was how to connect the inside and outside.'

A series of steel pillars emerges from the concrete base of the house, partially submerged in the ground, and these pillars support prefabricated timber-panel walls. Between the concrete and the timber is a band of glass, which offers a strong link between inside and out while also drawing in a richness of natural light.

Within the ground floor, the living spaces are open-plan, offering an impression of space and a free flow of light. These spaces revolve around a double-height central atrium, where internal windows from bedrooms and bathrooms on the floor above offer connections between the floors and additional borrowed light. The more intimate retreats on the upper storey are enriched by a series of windows to the exterior of varied sizes and positioning.

'While we wanted a certain separation between family life on the one hand and individual areas on the other, it was essential for us to connect both zones,' says Henning Wachsmuth, who runs a specialist IT recruitment company with his wife. 'So we needed a connecting element and the central atrium came up. It also helped create a sense of generosity in a very small house.'

The use of prefabricated panels – with high insulation standards – cut down on construction time as well as resources, with the house being built in just four months. It features a green roof and rainwater recycling, while the underfloor heating is fed by a ground source heat pump. Energy bills for the compact house are minimal.

'You can only create a good project by offering a space that provides a certain special kind of atmosphere to the user,' says Schönberg. 'So the focus was on using green technology where we could, but that alone would not have satisfied our architectural ambitions.'

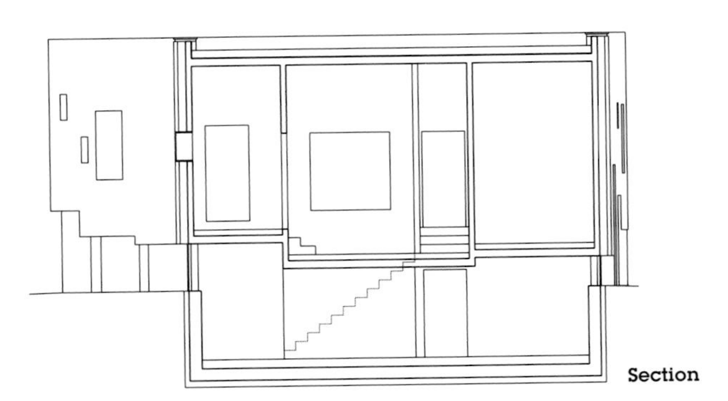

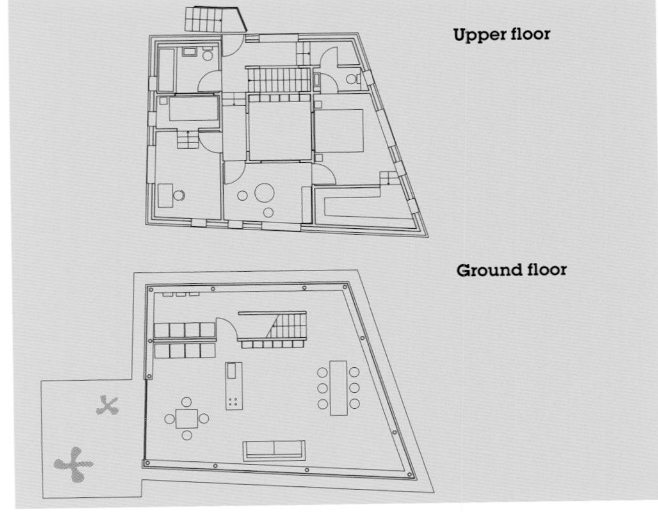

Pages 88–91 All the living spaces on both storeys of the house circulate around a central double-height atrium.

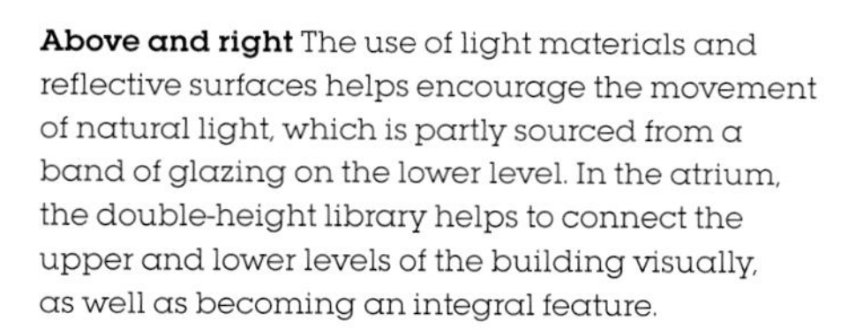

Above and right The use of light materials and reflective surfaces helps encourage the movement of natural light, which is partly sourced from a band of glazing on the lower level. In the atrium, the double-height library helps to connect the upper and lower levels of the building visually, as well as becoming an integral feature.

Aston Martin
DAS GROSSE
NEUBAUWELT
GARY LARSON

Opposite and this page In the kitchen and breakfast area (opposite), a large sliding door opens out onto the terrace. 'During the summer we open the sliding door more or less permanently, which shifts the centre of family activity to the terrace and gives us an enjoyable mix of inside and outside living,' says Henning Wachsmuth. On the upper level of the house (right), space-saving measures such as the elevated bed work around shifts in floor level, which are partly to do with creating visual connections with the atrium and lower level while also offering privacy when needed. The use of internal windows, complementing traditional external glazing, helps the flow of natural light throughout.

The irregular, sculpted form – coated in cement boards in green and white – allows light to penetrate deep into the body of the house itself.

KING RESIDENCE, SANTA MONICA, CA, USA

JOHN FRIEDMAN
ALICE KIMM
ARCHITECTS

A great deal of thought was given to the positioning of the King Residence on its unusual wedge-shaped corner plot in Santa Monica. The new house replaces a 1950s building that sat right in the middle of the site, which is clipped by a roadway to one side, so eroding the standard rectangular plan. Architects John Friedman and Alice Kimm worked on a number of possible permutations before deciding, with their clients, to reject the traditional American pattern of a front garden and back yard and positioned the new house at the very rear of the site. This created a large, open front lawn and an outward-looking aspect to the street, with the design of the exterior dominated by a large contemporary front porch. The orientation of the L-shaped house also makes the very best of the available light.

'The area gets good sun and the house is half a mile from the beach, so it also gets a good breeze,' says John Friedman. 'If you orientate the building correctly and open the house to the breeze then it's certainly not as challenging as building out in the desert or somewhere more extreme.'

The design of the two-storey home for Matt and Erin King and their two sons draws in sunlight through a series of techniques, as well as integrating natural ventilation methods. The irregular, sculpted form – coated in cement boards in green and white – allows light to penetrate deep into the body of the house itself, assisted by tall panels of floor-to-ceiling glazing. Sliding glass doors allow a fluid relationship between the porch and the main open-plan living area while also allowing sunlight to flood in.

'The house gets morning light, which warms up the house, and then is more protected from the afternoon sun,' Friedman says. 'The skylights in the house also help, and we have used them pushed up against white-painted internal walls so that the walls help bounce light back into the room.'

Skylights provide additional light in areas such as the kitchen, master bathroom and stairwell, where an operable skylight can also be used to vent rising hot air on warmer days. Internal doorways are made with frosted glass to allow light to pass through, while most rooms are enriched by drawing in light from windows looking out to different aspects, making the most of the passage of the sun through the day.

On the upper level, a recessed terrace also helps pull light deep into the home – particularly the master bedroom – while acting as a more private alternative outdoor space. This terrace is partially protected from the midday sun by a canopy, but one that is punctured, allowing a choice between sunshine and shade.

The house also incorporates a number of other eco-friendly elements. The pool by the front porch can help in cooling the house, benefiting from the evaporative effect of the water. The planting is all drought-resistant and low in water use, as selected by Erin King, a landscape designer. But the most striking element of the house – beyond the reinvention of the traditional front porch – remains the rich quality of sunlight that enlivens it throughout.

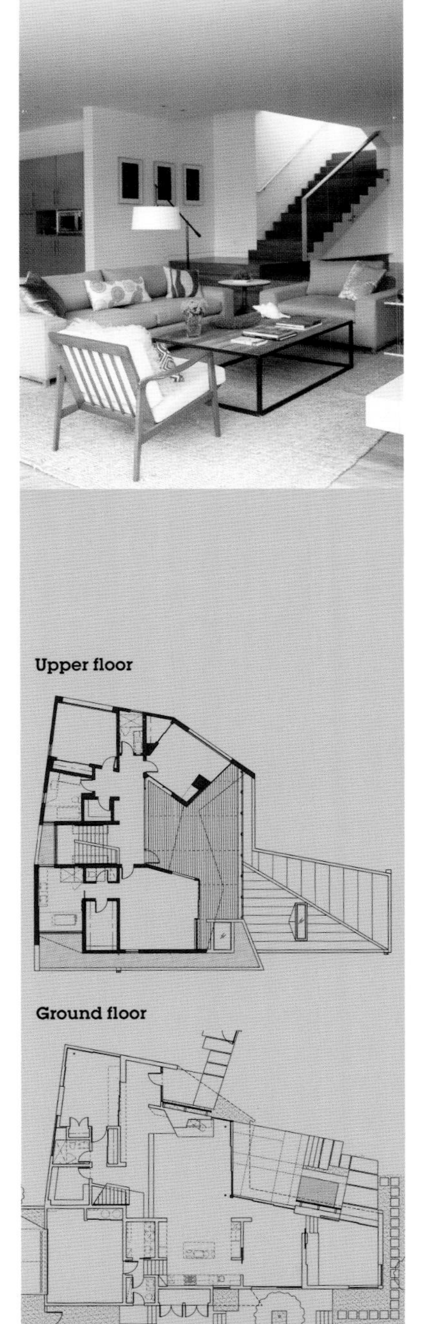

Pages 96–99 The King Residence benefits from a high quality of natural light, while the open plan of the main living spaces helps light to circulate freely. Key to this success is the way in which light enters from different aspects and sources, including glazed skylights and light wells.

Above and opposite The irregular plan of the house, with elements pushing outwards, introduces light from a variety of sources, like a plant pushing towards the sun. The deck on the upper level, indented into the overall outline, helps bring light into the bedrooms, while its punctured canopy allows options for shade and mitigates the noonday sunlight.

This multi-faceted triple skin can easily be adapted ... creating a high degree of flexibility to cope with a variety of weather conditions and temperatures.

MARIE SHORT HOUSE, KEMPSEY, NSW, AUSTRALIA

GLENN MURCUTT

The renowned Australian architect Glenn Murcutt is much respected for his sensitive understanding of the particular conditions of each and every site he builds upon. This was very much the case with his approach to the design of a house for client Marie Short in the rural farming community of Kempsey, New South Wales, around five hours' drive north of Sydney.

The project marked Murcutt's first commission for a country house and was highly influential in the evolution of his work. It also became a very personal project, as Murcutt later bought the house from Short to serve as his own country escape, extending the building to suit his needs and those of his family.

The house sits within around 640 acres of farmland, with a river forming part of the border of the farm. The climate is subtropical, so it is warm and temperate with high humidity and significant rainfall. In the heat of summer the farm benefits from cool breezes coming in from the coast to the north-east, but during the winter cold winds come in from the west. Murcutt understood all these conditions perfectly – as well as the movement of the sun – before designing the house.

'I knew the site backwards,' he says. 'I'd been going up there for a year and a half and understood the weather patterns, the rain, the wind. They were very important things to be aware of. We have always got rain, which makes the landscape rather lush and English in some ways.'

The building was designed in the form of two parallel but interconnecting timber-framed structures, slightly staggered in formation. They are raised up slightly off the ground to help protect the house from rainstorms, as well as offering some protection from wildlife such as snakes and allowing cooling breezes to pass beneath the house in summer.

The principal living spaces are positioned in the pavilion facing north, which benefits from the northern light as well as those cool breezes from the coast. For the external walls, Murcutt created a layered effect of three separate elements: an inner layer of flexible louvres, followed by a mesh insect screen and, finally, a more robust aluminium slatted screen, which can also be adjusted. This multi-faceted triple skin can easily be adapted in a series of combinations to open or close the walls, creating a high degree of flexibility to cope with a variety of weather conditions and temperatures. Roof lights admit extra sunlight in select parts of the house, with the addition of blinds for further flexibility. Each of the parallel pavilions also has a large and sheltered veranda contained within the overall outline of the building, with sliding glass walls separating them from the interiors while still allowing a through flow of light.

The design of the Marie Short House promotes the use of natural light, natural cooling and powerful connections with a dramatic landscape, all with the lightest of touches. 'It is a very special place for me,' says Murcutt. 'Some people who have been here have said that it's my paradise.'

Ground floor

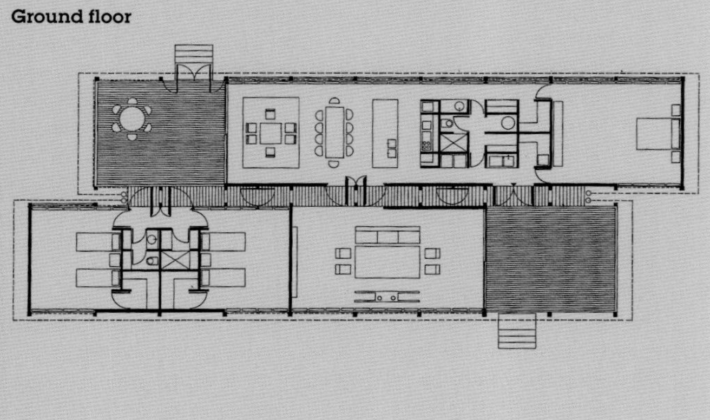

Pages 102–05 The form and design of the Marie Short House have proved inspirational and have been much imitated. A key aspect of its beauty and character is the way in which it interacts with the surrounding landscape. For Murcutt the house is a highly personal retreat. 'On any one day we have up to twenty kangaroos around the house and eight or nine wallabies,' he says. 'We have a beautiful lake fed by springs, and in the summer we get the perfume of water lilies carried over by the breeze.'

Left and below The interiors are warmed by the timber finishes and the natural light, which is drawn in from large skylights and long, transparent stretches of a triple skin made up of glass louvres, mesh insect screens and aluminium slatted blinds. This skin allows a fine degree of control over sunlight, solar gain and ventilation.

This page and opposite
Two verandas are integrated into the overall outline of the house, one at either end of the parallel pavilions that form the building. These verandas offer sheltered and shaded zones for eating and sitting in the open air while also drawing in light. The house can easily adapt to very different weather and light conditions by using natural methods to help cool, warm and illuminate it in all seasons. 'I knew exactly what to do here,' says Murcutt. 'The house released within me ideas that I'd been working on for a long time.'

3 | the material world

the material world

In recent years there has been a marked resurgence of interest in using natural materials for home-building, though often in fresh and unexpected ways. Architects and designers may have been influenced by traditional vernacular architecture to some degree but have also looked to the lessons of the gentle Modernists such as Alvar Aalto and Frank Lloyd Wright who advocated a more organic approach to design, while making the most of the rich textures and character of natural materials such as timber, clay, brick and stone.

It is the idea of character as much as the issue of sustainability that brings architects and designers back to such materials. Often they become part of houses that are strikingly modern and may be formally unusual or even experimental. The intrinsic wealth and grain of natural construction enlivens these houses while helping them relate all the better to the landscape and surroundings in which they sit.

In part, this resurgence can be seen as one element of a reaction to a late twentieth-century emphasis on conformist architecture, which produced cloned housing estates of little or no architectural interest, often made largely of concrete and steel. At the same time, so many urban buildings – from office blocks to hotels – seemed to default towards familiar ideas of construction and featureless façades of glass or metallic panels. It was not so much that these buildings were minimalist – which could, at best, involve a refocusing on the value and character of materials within a pared-down environment – but that they were simply bland and depressing.

The revival of interest in reinterpreting natural materials can be viewed as part of a more general shift back towards pattern, texture, decoration and formal experiment – away, in other words, from bland conformity and a regulation palette of materials. Increasingly, architects have begun to experiment with dynamic forms, colours and experimental surfaces and skins. Others have placed more importance on a simpler, more organic approach, using timber, stone and earth construction in creating homes of character and individuality.

Regional Sourcing

But while the revival of interest in more traditional and natural materials can be welcomed – for many different reasons – it is also true that the growing emphasis on sustainability and green issues has made the business of choosing the 'right' materials increasingly complex. It has become easy to tie oneself in knots when making such decisions as so many different factors come into play, with aesthetics only one factor in the equation.

To be environmentally conscious we must really consider elements such as the potential damage caused to the environment by the extraction and processing of construction materials, as well as the embodied energy used in fabricating these materials to the point where they are ready for use. One thinks of concerns about aluminium, for instance, and worries over the impact of its processing – which releases significant quantities of carbon dioxide – and possible pollution. We also need to think about the associated mileage – by land, sea or air – that any materials might accumulate during the course of their production and through delivery to site.

Once upon a time, of course, it was all so much simpler. Traditionally, the majority of houses and buildings were made of the raw materials most easily available locally or regionally. For large parts of Austria, Scandinavia or New England, that might well be timber. For many regions of France, the Cotswolds or the Lake District in England, it would be stone. In countless regions of the world, building blocks would come from the ground itself in the form of adobe or *pisé* (rammed earth). Inevitably,

Pages 110–11 The Quail Hill House, Long Island, USA, by Bates Masi Architects.

Opposite Architect Barton Myers used a system of garage doors in the master bedroom of his home in Toro Canyon, CA, where the relationship between outside and inside is highly fluid. The house also explores striking contrasts between natural materials and landscaping and industrial design elements.

The intrinsic wealth and grain of natural construction enlivens these houses while helping them relate all the better to the landscape and surroundings in which they sit.

Above and opposite At this holiday home in Portsea, on the Mornington Peninsula in Australia, architect Chris Connell used rammed earth to create a home rich in natural texture and character, responding to the clients' desire for 'modern earthiness'.

such natural selection helped give rise to vernacular flavours and regional architectural identity, as well as diverse character. Even the tones and shades of fired brick varied from region to region, depending on the clay mix being used.

In many respects, this traditional approach to material choices helped to tie a building into its surroundings. A barn is one of the most beautiful and practical of building types and seems intimately bound to the landscape that helped to produce it in the first place. Traditionally barns were built with the most easily available materials to hand and made use of local topography to provide shelter from the elements. A bank barn, for instance, might be pushed into the side of a hill and made of stone or flint picked out of the fields nearby as they were cleared for cultivation. Or timber might be felled for a wood-clad agricultural shed. It was about using the most easily available materials with the least labour – or energy.

That is not to say that all buildings were made this way or should be approached in the same way again. The castle and cathedral in my hometown were built of creamy French stone imported from Caen in the twelfth century. The world has changed many times over since then, and of course we do not want to be limited to local sources when we build our homes.

Yet, as with so many issues related to sustainability, common sense will inevitably push us towards sourcing as locally and regionally as possible. The allure of a beautiful hardwood cladding, for instance, may not make so much sense – even when it's sourced from an approved and carefully managed forest – if it has to travel halfway around the world to reach the building site.

In building his own rammed-earth home in Schlins, Austrian architect Martin Rauch (see page 142) sourced the vast majority of the raw earth he needed from the site itself, while also sourcing timber beams locally. Yet the house is striking in its modernity, with great attention paid to aesthetics and character.

Similarly, English architect Vicky Thornton (see page 238) sourced locally as far as possible when building her holiday home in south-western France. The limestone walls of the lower level were recycled from a demolished stone building in the region, while the timber frame and chestnut cladding for the upper level were also regionally produced.

Glass, Concrete and Stone

Contemporary architects are reinterpreting natural materials – sensitively sourced from accredited suppliers – in striking ways and original forms. Certain regions, such as Vorarlberg in Austria, have become known for the way in which they have built upon local traditions – such as the timber mountain house – and reinvented them for modern living.

This does not mean, of course, that modern technology and other materials do not have a place in new natural homes. Obviously, glass is an essential element, and its insulating qualities have been vastly improved in recent years. Steel frames and beams, despite the embodied energy involved and their rising cost, are still part of the standard building tool kit, with recycled steel becoming more widely available.

It is concrete that might provide one of the most intense debating points when it comes to choosing between building materials. With its cement root, concrete has been widely attacked by environmentalists on a number of different grounds. Most serious of all are the large amounts of energy needed to manufacture cement and the high levels of carbon-dioxide

emissions involved in the process. As a staple of the construction industry, then, concrete has been widely criticized.

But for limited use, many environmentally aware architects are still drawn to concrete, especially for foundations and flooring. This is not just because of its inherent structural advantages, ease of use and hard-wearing practicality, but also because of its high thermal mass. Concrete floors, especially, can help to maintain an even temperature within a building, keeping it cool in summer and warm in winter. By being slow to heat up or to cool down, concrete acts as a regulator.

Concrete, like brick, also has the advantage of being long-lasting, something that does need to be taken into account when weighing up the eco-credentials of different kinds of materials. Brick-built homes from the Victorian and Georgian eras are still very much part of the built environment in countries like Britain, where brick buildings have often proved to be more enduring and adaptable than – for example – houses and apartment blocks from the 1960s and 1970s, which have already had to be replaced.

Meanwhile, the cement industry – like the paint industry, the brick industry and others – has been seeking to reduce its carbon footprint and environmental impact.

Ultimately, the choice of materials is allied to the process of design itself and dictated not just by issues of sustainability but also by aesthetic and architectural needs, as well as cost and practicality. A house is a complex kit of parts and one that often evolves and changes over time, as well as needing care and maintenance. A well-built, well-made and adaptable home is always going to be preferable – on any criteria – to a home that is impractical and in need of constant updating or even replacement.

Prefabrication

One growing area of concern, when it comes to sustainability, is the wastefulness and inefficiency of a regular building site. The idea of bringing labour and disparate materials to a site day by day, with all the transport involved, along with the time and waste involved in daily construction, has spurred growing interest in prefabrication.

This has seen an increasing demand for structural insulated panels (SIPs), which are essentially factory-made wall systems of reconstituted timber, lightweight and hard-wearing but complete with a high level of thermal insulation. At the same time, using pre-ordered and factory-made SIPs can radically speed up construction time and reduce wastage. On every level they are seen as environmentally friendly.

Prefabrication is taken even further with the concept of the modular home – creating a series of factory-made units that can be slotted together on site on a prepared foundation. As far as possible, these modules are factory-fitted with flooring, walls, service ducts, insulation and other elements, which vastly reduces the labour and delivered materials needed on the building site itself. These modules are transported by truck and rapidly slot together, leaving a ready-made home, suitable for final fitting and connection to services.

Modular systems such as Huf Haus and Pagano have been around for some time. But in recent years, a number of architectural firms – such as Buckley Gray Yeoman, Marmol Radziner (see page 120) and Alchemy Architects – have developed new modular systems that are also designed to be environmentally aware. These units can be tailored or used in different combinations to create homes with a greater degree of individuality although still factory-produced with each module fitting on to a flatbed lorry.

Above At the Said House in Vaucluse, NSW, Australia, architects Design King Company used stone cladding and recycled materials to bring a sense of sculpted warmth, depth and delight to a home that is strikingly modern in form.

Opposite Architect Cheong Yew Kuan created a series of interconnected pavilions, partially open to nature, at his home in Ubud, Bali. Terracotta tiles on the walls contrast with concrete ceilings, timber, water and the surrounding greenery in a carefully composed melange of textures and hues.

'Prefabrication gives us ways of actually making a house in a way that uses less energy and resources. In terms of being eco-friendly, there is no question that building modules in the factory is less consumptive than building on site.'

Above A deep Japanese-style timber bath graces a cedar-clad house designed by architect Andrew Lister in Auckland, New Zealand.

Marmol Radziner have developed a series of prefabricated modular homes – using recycled steel frames – beginning with Leo Marmol's own family holiday home near Palm Springs. Marmol points out that, unlike early twentieth-century experiments with modular buildings, the design input is exceptionally high and the green aspects of the building process are a powerful marketing tool.

'Prefabrication gives us ways of actually making a house in a way that uses less energy and resources,' he says. 'In terms of being eco-friendly, there is no question that building modules in the factory is less consumptive than building on site. This is now the marketing approach and that's what sells modular houses. Our goal in the end is not just to sell a prefabricated house but a beautiful, modern, sustainable lifestyle. Prefabrication is a means to get there.'

Natural Selection

Undoubtedly, sustainability is having a huge impact on the development of the modern home and of architecture overall. Inevitably, this growing eco-awareness will have a great effect on the way we build and the materials we use. But it would be wrong to see this shift as limiting. It simply means that we will give more thought to the materials we choose, the way they are made and where they come from. Even materials that might not have such good press in environmental terms – aluminium, for example – may still be feasible to use if we can source them in a recycled form.

Almost inevitably, however, there is a return to more traditional and natural materials, especially timber, which many now see as a win-win material as long as it's sourced from managed and sustainable forestry. Woodland, of course, captures CO_2 from the environment and releases oxygen, creating valuable carbon stores. If we then use this material for construction, while replanting, we involve ourselves in an environmentally friendly process.

At the same time none of us wants to endorse the destructive harvesting of hardwood or rainforest timbers that are so hard to replace and replant. There's no doubt that when using tropical hardwoods such as Brazilian ipe or common Asian teak, extra care is needed in checking their origins. Also, this wood should be used more sparingly than more readily available and faster-growing timbers.

Perhaps the key point is that putting great thought into material choices and being environmentally aware do not have to involve a cap on imagination or creativity. Our homes will not be poorer for paying greater attention to these things, but richer. It is, in a sense, a new kind of organic architecture but one that is not allied to any particular design movement forcing us into a single aesthetic or stylistic direction. The organic approach to building our homes should be liberating, never confining.

SUMMARY

General

* Source materials and labour locally or regionally wherever possible.
* Consider recycled materials, such as recycled steel, aluminium and brick or reclaimed stone or hardwood.
* Select materials according to local climate and conditions, as well as aesthetics and sustainability.
* Ensure that any exterior or exposed materials will weather appropriately and can be easily maintained, bearing in mind that there is no such thing as a maintenance-free home.
* Pay attention to the content and toxicity of paints, coatings and sealants. The use of inappropriate coatings can undermine the merits of carefully selected materials, in terms of both sustainability and healthy living.
* Look at prefabrication technology and techniques as ways of reducing construction time and transportation costs to site. When using timber-frame prefabrication or timber-panel construction systems, the ecological benefits will be even more pronounced.
* Think about the importance of material choices in defining the character and feel of the home and whether or not your selection conveys a sense of warmth and texture. Materials play a key role in establishing the mood of particular rooms and spaces in the house.
* Look at the way different materials will work together and whether they will complement one another or clash.
* Avoid monotony. Overuse of a single material, especially within the home, can lead to a visual famine. Balance simplicity with a need for variety and interest.
* Do not be afraid of using colour and expressing yourself through materials and finishes. Crisp white boxes can be dull and characterless, no matter how worthily sustainable they are. Exercise your right to experiment and create a home that suits your own temperament.
* Consider planting trees, shrubs and greenery within landscaping around the home to help 'offset' the use of materials and embodied energy in the construction of a home.
* Pay attention to high visibility surfaces, particularly cladding and roofing. The finish of a pitched roof, for instance, will have a high impact and shape the character of the building dramatically.
* Do not be afraid of bespoke solutions. Look at tailoring materials, such as cladding, to create a more individual and unique home.

Timber

* Source timber from approved suppliers using sustainable forestry in order to be assured of the many green benefits of timber construction.
* Consider the effect of your local climate and weather on the timbers you use, especially for exterior cladding. Consider investing in timber that will respond well to local conditions.
* Avoid any cheaply processed timbers that may have been treated with harmful or even toxic chemicals.
* Remember that timber is a highly adaptable and malleable material that can be shaped according to your needs and wishes. Shingles, for instance, are one alternative to standard timber cladding.
* Common choices for cladding timber might include Douglas fir, red cedar and larch.
* Ensure that only porous treatments are applied to timber cladding so that the timber can 'breathe' and thereby last longer. Similarly, ensure that timber coats are protected from damp with ventilation gaps and effective rainwater drainage.
* Take the effect of weathering on timber cladding into account – timber such as oak and larch will naturally grey over time.
* Timber is a natural material that does need care and maintenance. Ensure that timber building coats are checked periodically for damage and deterioration.
* Investigate prefabricated timber building systems with ready fitted layers of insulation, such as structural insulated panels (SIPs), which could cut down on construction costs and time spent on site.
* Check on whether timber structures, cladding and finishes need to be given fire-retardant coatings.
* Timber is a relatively lightweight material, so may be particularly well suited to areas where shallow foundations are required or where the house needs to be elevated above ground level, to avoid flood risk, for instance.
* Timber on its own has a poor thermal mass; high-quality layers of insulation will always be needed to boost the thermal performance of a timber-walled home.

Concrete

* Concrete floor pads and foundations have strong practical advantages and high thermal mass, despite the negative aspects of cement production with its high CO_2 emissions.
* The production of cement, one of the prime ingredients of concrete, is without doubt a high energy process, involving high levels CO_2 emissions.
* Concrete is highly flexible in its use, but it is also difficult to recycle or adapt once fixed in place, so look at using it sparingly as well as being open to alternatives.
* Consider offsetting the use of concrete or other materials with high embodied energy – such as metal cladding – with the use of more benign natural materials elsewhere, as well as additional planting, whether in the garden or as a green roof.
* Look at softening the raw quality of concrete with the use of more natural materials such as timber and stone. Such contrasts can be effective and seductive.
* Consider 'customizing' concrete finishes where appropriate with pigments or polishing and also patinas, such as the outward imprint of timber boards on concrete surfaces when used as temporary box moulds for poured concrete.

Other Materials

* When using metals such as steel and aluminium, look at recycled products. Seek to limit the use of non-recycled metal construction materials.
* Metals, more than most materials, have a long and sometimes complex sourcing and production 'history' behind them. Mining, transportation and high energy production techniques all add to the high embodied energy with metal construction materials, which needs to be balanced with their benefits, strength and versatility.
* Steelwork frames and beams are an accepted, familiar and sometimes essential part of the house-building tool kit. But there are alternatives, such as timber frames.
* Steel and other metals can be used more benignly – despite their initial embodied production energy – if part of a prefabricated construction system, which might reduce construction time and transport costs.
* Weigh up the longevity of materials such as brick against the energy needed to produce the materials in the first place. Clay bricks have a powerful track record in homes that continue to be adaptable and flexible.
* Look at using recycled bricks where possible, or locally fired bricks that have an intrinsic vernacular quality, made with regional methods and materials.
* Be open to 'revival' building techniques, such as rammed earth and other forms of earth construction.
* Be sensitive to, rather than obsessive about, the pros and cons of every material choice. Consider materials that are suited to the site and climate and have an established vernacular presence in your area, but without feeling constrained by traditional styles or aesthetics.

'If you are going to experiment, then the first experiment should always be upon yourself.'

DESERT HOUSE, DESERT HOT SPRINGS, COACHELLA VALLEY, CA, USA

MARMOL RADZINER

During the summer months, temperatures in the Coachella Valley, near Palm Springs, can reach between 100 and 120 degrees Fahrenheit. In the winter the days are much milder, but the nights can be biting cold. This is a place of extremes, with a wild and enticing kind of beauty. And this is where architect Leo Marmol chose to build a holiday home for his family – the first in a sequence of prefabricated Marmol Radziner houses.

'If you are going to experiment, then the first experiment should always be on yourself so that you can make sure you can actually do it,' says Marmol. 'We were the guinea pigs with the Desert House and our prefabrication process was refined from there.'

Marmol's interest in prefabrication has been partly driven by the sustainable aspects of building modular homes in a factory, where the waste and inefficiencies of traditional building sites can be vastly reduced. Recycled steel was used to create a series of frames for the ten separate modules that make up the Desert House, with each module fitted out as far as practical before delivery to the site. This included polished concrete floors and cabinetwork.

The ten modules – four interior units and six exterior ones – were delivered on trucks and erected over the course of a day on a prepared concrete foundation. The modules gently cantilever over the foundation so the base seems to disappear, thus giving the impression of a floating home. The building was carefully positioned to take account of both the track of the sun and the mesmerizing views of Mt San Jacinto and the other peaks surrounding the valley.

'We used outdoor living spaces to help shield the interiors from the sunlight,' says Marmol, who shares the house with his wife Alisa Becket and their daughter. 'We always integrate a good deal of outdoor living space.'

Natural cross-ventilation helps to cool the single-storey house via a series of opening glass doors complemented by a skylight which helps to vent hot air. Concrete floor slabs with high thermal mass also help to regulate the inside temperature. Insulation qualities are high in the modular walls, while the large banks of glazing use low-emissivity, argon-filled, triple-paned glass.

The energy requirements of the house – in a region rich in renewable energy from countless wind turbines – are partly met by solar panels on the flat roof. Marmol had a well dug so that water needs could also be met on site.

While providing a retreat from Los Angeles for Marmol and his family, the Desert House suggested the possibilities – in terms of both sustainability and aesthetics – of a new breed of modular home. Lessons learned from the experience of this pioneering prototype have since fed through into a high-end range of Marmol Radziner modular prefabs.

Pages 120–25 The modular formation of the house includes a series of verandas and decks, with canopies and projecting roofs that shade and protect the interiors. In essence, the house is a series of interconnected pavilions opening out to the landscape. 'I like the house in the summer,' says Marmol, 'because you have to slow down. You can't continue at a city pace when you are there. It forces you to relax.'

Above Many internal fixtures, fittings and fitted elements were created within the prefabricated modules at the factory. Much of the loose furniture was also designed by Marmol Radziner.

Above Materials used in the construction of the house include recycled steel and sustainably forested timber. In the bathroom, a skylight over the bath helps to introduce natural light.

'Madrid can also be a very windy city, as well as hot, so we needed an intelligent ventilation system.'

LAS ROZAS HOUSE, MADRID, SPAIN

ABALOS+ SENTKIEWICZ ARQUITECTOS

Sited close to an oak wood on the outskirts of Madrid, Marina Collazo's home was designed with a sensitive eye for the surrounding environment. 'I wanted to leave a minimal trace,' says Collazo, a television producer. 'In many aspects of my life, I am trying to consume less resources and generate less waste, so when I began the big project of building my own house, I tried as hard as I could to respect the environment.'

Collazo had not always wanted to build her own home, but – having lived in an apartment building at the heart of Madrid and in a semi-detached house – she decided that she wanted a stand-alone home for herself, her husband and her daughter. Finding a suitable site took around three years. Then she turned to architect Iñaki Ábalos of Abalos+Sentkiewicz in Madrid.

The building was created with a steel frame coated in a highly insulated wall system topped with Viroc timber-particle boards, made from a mix of wood and cement, laid in vertical strips up the side of the cuboid building. These boards give the house heavy-duty protection from the elements, but also have a pleasing textured quality.

The house features a system of louvred shutters over the windows and doors, which help ventilate without the need for air conditioning. Cool air is drawn in at the bottom of the building and vented from the upper levels, keeping the house at a comfortable temperature even in the height of summer, when it can reach 104 degrees in the city. Pushing the house into the site by partially submerging the lower ground-floor level helped to maximize thermal insulation.

'We also decided to make the ceilings of the rooms upstairs really high, as has always been the case in traditional Spanish architecture, so that the hot air rises and vents outside,' says Ábalos. 'But Madrid can also be a very windy city, as well as hot, so we needed an intelligent ventilation system. From the outset, our client made it clear that she wanted an ecologically friendly home and this fitted naturally with the principles of good design.'

The idea of flexibility and choice continues through into the layout of the house. Day-to-day living spaces are on the ground floor, with the main bedrooms at the top of the house. A modest roof terrace has also been integrated into the outline, while a simply designed paved terrace and pool complement the main building. Around this, landscaping has been kept to a minimum.

The house at Las Rozas is very different from its more conventional neighbours, having become a sculpted, almost abstract object in the landscape. Yet it is also a highly respectful, practical and flexible family home.

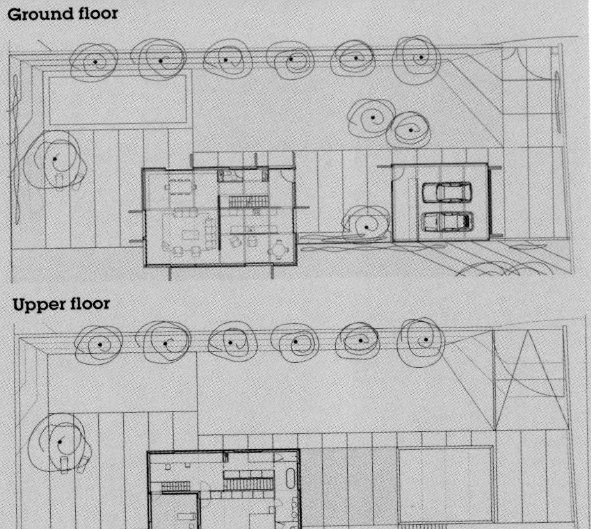

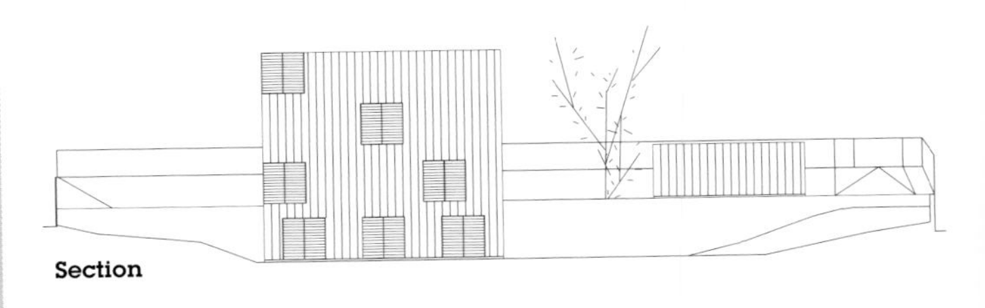

Section

Pages 128–31 A flexible system of louvred shutters over all the windows and doorways can be used to open up or close down the house and provide varying degrees of shade. The vents can also be used as an integral part of the natural ventilation system, which does away with any need for air conditioning, even at the height of summer.

Above A key element of the design of the house is its flexibility. 'The organization of the house is very simple: everyday living is on the ground floor, the parents are on the first floor, the children on the lower level. But the plan of the house allows for all kinds of changes,' says architect Iñaki Ábalos.

Above Partially submerging a section of the house helps to improve its thermal quality and keeps it cool, assisted by the use of a concrete floor pad with a high thermal mass. The underfloor heating system used to warm the house in winter can be run in reverse to aid cooling in summer.

'When we use regional timber, we can see the trees growing around us …. It's about appreciating the chain of production and having a sense of connection.'

LUTZ HOUSE, BREGENZ, VORARLBERG, AUSTRIA

PHILIP LUTZ ARCHITEKTUR

The Lutz House sits on its mountainside site like some extraordinary sculpted and crafted object. It has a gentle, almost sinuous quality as well as an aerodynamic vitality, like a stranded ship. But at the same time this is a building tied to the landscape – and the forestry that provides it with a dramatic backdrop – by the use of natural materials and a coating of locally sourced pine shingles.

'The shingles are in local timber that is untreated,' says architect and resident Philip Lutz, who shares the house with his wife Annette and their three children. 'It's very easily available and affordable, and we have also used pine for the interiors.

'We thought about using a copper cladding but decided that it would be too unfriendly and alien. It was very easy to shingle the irregular form of the house compared to using a metal cladding. The shingles are flexible and it gives the house a hand-crafted feeling. It is a modern house but very rooted in the local tradition.'

The house is situated at the edge of Bregenz, the capital of the province of Vorarlberg, not far from the borders with Switzerland and Germany. Positioned on the slopes of the Pfänder, with the mountain's cable car passing overhead, the Lutz residence makes the most of this extraordinary site on the borders between town and country, with spectacular views over Bregenz and Lake Constance below.

Lutz and his wife bought the site with an existing 1980s house of poor design – its main living spaces on the lower level wasted the best of the views – and badly orientated in terms of light. The family lived in the existing house for five years before embarking on a radical reinvention. During this time Lutz was able to study the site with care and truly understand the movement of light and the effect of the changing seasons.

The new house was built on the recycled foundations and footprint of the old one. However, the structure was twisted around to take full advantage of the light and the views while turning its back on a logging track and footpath. The key living spaces – in an open-plan layout – were positioned on the upper level, with a dramatic cantilevered terrace alongside for summer dining. The bedrooms and Annette's studio are on the ground level.

The tapered form helps soften the home, providing a more pleasing alternative to a regular rectangular shape. Within, as well as pine, Lutz selected wide fir floorboards full of character from a timber yard just across the German border. The textures and tone of the wood offer a contrast with the highly contemporary flavour of the large expanses of glazing, which bathe the interiors with natural light.

'The house is not refined in every detail, which makes it more relaxed and informal,' Lutz says. 'Everything does not have to be perfect and the timber gives the house warmth. When we use regional timber, we can see the trees growing around us. I prefer working with a timber workshop that I know and where I can understand where the wood has come from. It's about appreciating the chain of production and having a sense of connection rather than just ordering metal sheets from a catalogue.'

Upper floor

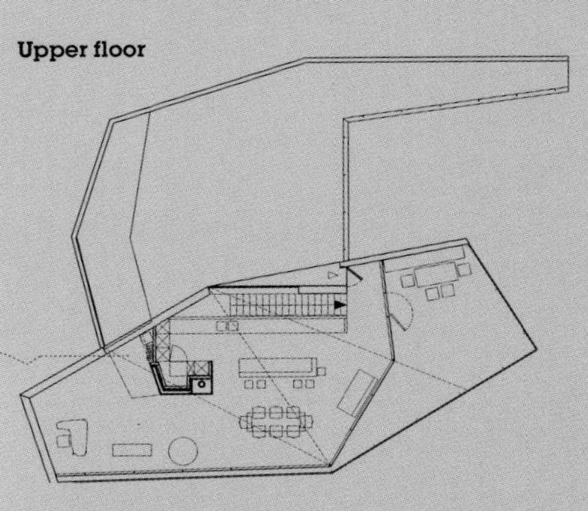

Ground floor

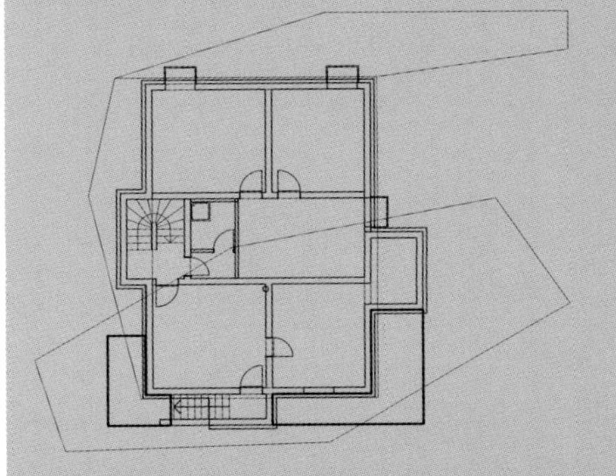

Pages 134–37 Fir and pine timbers warm the interiors of the house, while the irregular, undulating form of the ceiling helps soften the lines of the key living spaces on the upper level. The building is coated in a skin of pine shingles, also sourced locally.

Above The wide fir floorboards were found in a timber yard just across the German border. 'It's like a medieval floor,' says Lutz. 'The boards are not strictly parallel but long and irregular. So we slotted them together like a jigsaw puzzle.'

Above The kitchen is a bespoke design by Philip Lutz. It and the living area open out onto a large elevated terrace, complete with outdoor dining table, with inspirational views across Lake Constance. The banks of glazing along the open-plan living spaces of the upper level also make the most of this vista.

Above and opposite The pine shingles will acquire character and patina as they grey with age. Exposed parts of the house will weather more quickly, lending it a variegated coat. This is part of the building's unique and ever-changing personality. 'Sustainability is not just about building a box on a meadow with zero energy loss but about acceptance and love of a building,' says Lutz. 'If you love it then you will care for it.'

'The house grew slowly and we had plenty of time to plan details and think about different elements. That time was important for the development of the house.'

RAUCH HOUSE, SCHLINS, VORARLBERG, AUSTRIA

MARTIN RAUCH / ROGER BOLTSHAUSER

The raw materials for Martin Rauch's home come from the earth itself. Rauch has been working in rammed-earth construction since the 1980s, basing himself in the scenic Austrian village of Schlins. Here he not only has his atelier – home to his company Lehm Ton Erde – but he has also put a wealth of experience to use in creating a striking, contemporary earth home.

Designed in collaboration with architect Roger Boltshauser, the Rauch House is sited on a sloping hillside on the edge of the village, with pasture beyond and views of the Wolgau Valley and Austrian Alps. Rauch's three-storey home, shared with his wife – ceramicist Marta Rauch-Debevec – and their two children, is pushed into the hillside, with a strong linear presence softened by the textures of the building itself and the discretion of the landscaping.

Around 85 per cent of the building, which is strengthened with locally sourced timber beams, is made from earth excavated from the site itself and then sifted and graded. Even stones removed during grading were reused for infill around the building and for landscaping work.

Fitting the construction of the house around other projects in Austria and abroad, the Rauch House was built over a period of three years, with rammed-earth walls constructed to a height of 10 feet at a time. These would be allowed to dry before adding another layer on top, with lines of clay tiles used between the layers to reinforce the walls.

'I was co-architect, contractor and client for this house, which is easier on the one hand but on the other hand you do need a vision,' says Rauch. 'We were only able to build when we had the time to spare from our other work. The house grew slowly and we had plenty of time to plan details and think about different elements. That time was important for the development of the house.'

The walls integrate layers of reed insulation, with a clay plaster finish for the interiors. Floors are also made of compacted earth that has been polished with wax, while Marta Rauch-Debevec and her son Sebastian Rauch collaborated on the design of striking bespoke clay tiles for the entrance hallway on the lower ground level and the master bedroom on the top level. Energy is provided by solar panels on the roof, a wood-burning stove in the kitchen (which helps heat the house as well as being used for cooking), plus a wood-pellet boiler, which is generally only used in the winter months.

'We are not zero carbon, but we do have very low energy use,' says Rauch. 'But that was not as important to us as building with materials that don't need so much primary energy in production or application. Also, there is no element of pollution – it is completely environmentally friendly and the materials can all be recycled. That's very important for the future. Everything that we are building now could have to be rebuilt in fifty or a hundred years' time, so the question of what will happen to all these materials – and how they could be recycled – is an important one.'

Ground floor

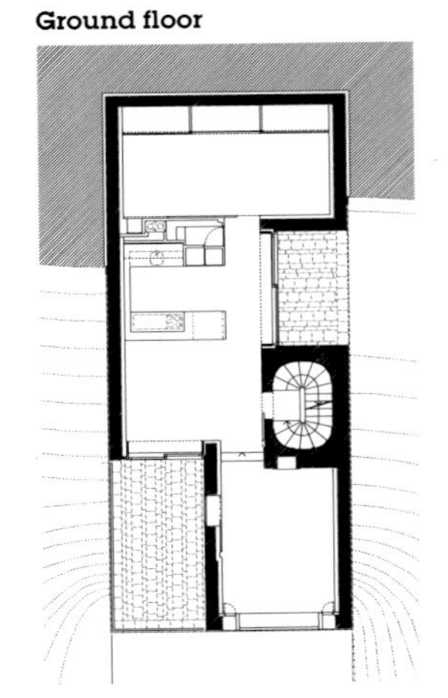

Middle floor

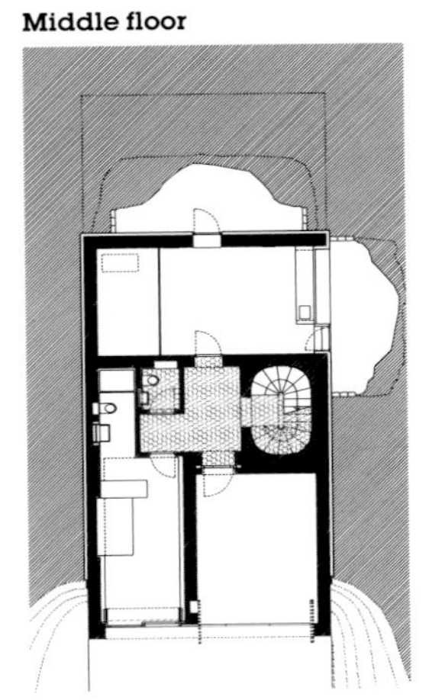

Top floor

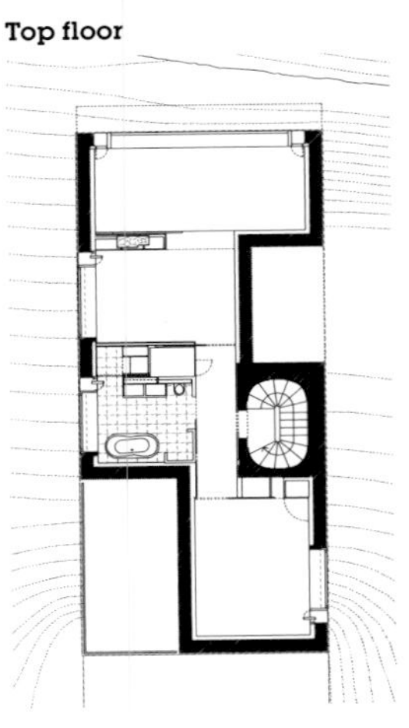

Pages 142–45 The raw layers of rammed earth used to build the house tell the long story of its construction. The structure literally grew from the ground, using materials excavated from the site to create it. In the entrance hall, bespoke ceramic tiles designed by Marta Rauch-Debevec and her son Sebastian create a crafted point of contrast with the earthen walls.

Opposite and this page Earth was used to create all the surfaces and finishes, inside and outside. 'You can build with natural materials like earth to a very high quality and with high aesthetics,' says Martin Rauch. 'The floors are earthen as well, made of compacted earth polished with wax and oil.'

Above As well as natural light and eco-friendly energy sources, the house is naturally ventilated, with timber hatches alongside the glazing.

Above The kitchen is a bespoke design by Martin Rauch. The oven runs on firewood and helps to heat the house. Plenty of storage space has been neatly woven into the design.

Pages 150–51 The master bedroom and bathroom are positioned on the upper floor of the house. The bathroom is enlivened with bespoke ceramic floor tiles designed by Marta Rauch-Debevec and son Sebastian, as well as ceramic wall tiles incorporating glass discs.

'Sustainability is not just an add-on but a factor as important as all the others and should be treated with equal attention.'

UTZON CABIN, TIBIRKE, DENMARK

KIM UTZON ARKITEKTER

The summer retreat that architect Kim Utzon created for himself and his family was – in a way – the fortunate product of recycling. Utzon had originally designed two compact prefabricated timber pavilions for a Scandinavian housing expo, but when his wife, Charlotte, saw the pavilions she realized that they would also make a perfect holiday retreat.

The Utzons began searching for a suitable site in Denmark or neighbouring Sweden before coming across some land in a rural spot some miles from the sea at Tibirke, around forty-five minutes north-west of Copenhagen. After the expo was over, the two pavilions were taken to the site by lorry, installed on prepared foundations and then linked by modest connecting structures. Later, a third pavilion in the same style was added to the house – which sits among meadow grass, with towering trees providing some shade – to offer the couple's grown-up son David a space of his own.

The pavilions, then, proved their flexibility. They were designed to be factory-made, with a sense of restraint and simplicity that led some at the expo to comment on their Japanese-seeming serenity as much as their Scandinavian aesthetic.

'Prefabrication has two advantages,' says Utzon. 'You have a more controlled environment during construction in a factory with less waste and no adverse weather conditions. So there is a more efficient use of time and materials, which in the end is more sustainable. If the transport expenditure is not out of balance then prefabrication is a greener alternative to traditional on-site construction.'

Each pavilion is clad in cedar boards and fitted with a vaulted zinc roof, with clerestory windows neatly tucked into the arches at either end to enhance the natural lighting and allow for an element of transparency. Within, the walls and ceilings are coated with beech ply panels while the floors are in limed Douglas fir.

'Although all the surfaces are timber, the house doesn't have an overwhelming wooden feeling because all the timber is different,' says Utzon. 'We wanted a simple, serviceable summer house that would withstand the Danish winter with as little upkeep as possible. I also wanted the house to blend into the site.'

Now that the cedar cladding and decking have silvered, the cabin has softened into the landscape. A wood-burning stove helps to warm it, while the furniture has been kept simple so as to fit with the relaxed, informal nature of the pavilions themselves. The family uses the cabin over the summer and at weekends, adopting a less complicated way of life compared to city living. 'As a small house it's better than I ever imagined,' says Utzon. 'Any house should respond to a site, the client and a brief, but it should also respond and contribute to our common environment. Sustainability is not just an add-on but a factor as important as all the others and should be treated with equal attention.'

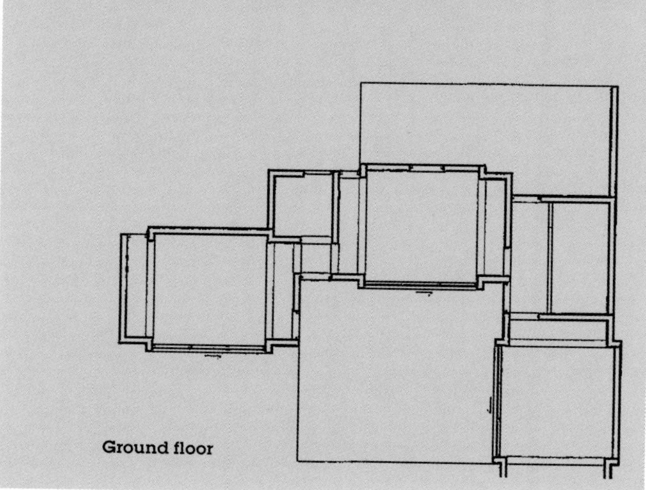

Pages 152–55 Although timber is so clearly the dominant material, the use of many different kinds and finishes of wood creates character and variety. The walls are in beech plywood and the fir floors have been lightened with lye and soap. The high, arched clerestory windows within the pavilions help show the grain and patina of the timber at its best.

This page and opposite
The pavilions open up to the surrounding landscape, and even the high windows frame views of the trees and greenery, whether in the living room or the master bedroom. 'The way that the light changes the feel of the place through the day is one of the special things about the house,' says Kim Utzon. 'My favourite time of day is waking up at sunrise and seeing the first light shining onto the ceiling.' The warm, natural simplicity of the design fits with the idea of creating an unpretentious, low-maintenance holiday home that can easily withstand the changing seasons.

4| indoor/outdoor living

indoor/outdoor living

'The more we connect to nature in the way we live, then the more responsible we are going to be about green decisions,' says architect Sebastian Mariscal. 'It's about establishing a different mindset.' The importance of this sense of connection between home and the natural world cannot be underestimated.

In many cities and growing urban centres, our gardens, parks and outdoor spaces have been under threat. In cities such as London, modest front gardens have been increasingly paved over to create offstreet parking. The rising value and scarcity of development sites in many urban areas has also seen sections of gardens sold off to create new homes, along with leftover pieces of land once thought too difficult or demanding to build upon. At the same time, developers have been tempted to create housing with inadequate gardens or exterior space as they have sought to maximize the number of homes built on new sites.

The dangers of inadequate outdoor space are many, with great implications for physical health, mental and social well-being, and the environmental impact of taking away the 'green lungs' provided by gardens and green spaces in congested, often polluted urban areas. One of the greatest problems is the resulting sense of disconnection between home and the natural world. In too many cities, it is possible to become quite alienated from nature – even from the impact of the changing seasons. From this disconnection, one can argue, comes the risk of a breakdown of understanding – particularly among children – about the natural world and its sublime processes and rhythms. If we don't feel that sense of daily connection, the risk is that we don't fully appreciate the beauty of nature and our own responsibility to care for the environment.

Even in a city centre, we should be able to create modest gardens and outdoor spaces with an inspirational aspect. Recently, there have been many encouraging design projects and schemes which suggest that there has been a shift towards a much greater appreciation of the importance of green space and easy-access outdoor living areas. In New York, the creation of a major new park in the form of the High Line project – which has seen a section of disused elevated railroad turned into a seductive new amenity space – is just one element of a concerted attempt at greening the city and providing a whole series of new parks. In Tokyo, planning guidance has been revised to encourage the creation of green spaces and planting within new developments, and this has led to an increased provision of roof gardens, terraces and green planted screens.

Within the design of the contemporary home, too, there is a renewed emphasis on the great value of outdoor space across the board, even on the tightest and most constrained of urban sites. This has led to an increase in the number of planted roof gardens, sunken courtyards, decks and terraces that seek to promote that life-affirming sense of connection with the natural world and all of the benefits this brings with it, including – one hopes – a greater sense of shared responsibility for protecting the environment around us.

Crossing Borders

The promotion of a fluid relationship between outdoors and in has been a key aspect of the evolving form and ethos of the home throughout the twentieth century. Advances in engineering, materials and design that allowed for curtain walls and banks of glazing not only permitted natural light to permeate the home but also created a level of transparency that allowed garden and landscape to become an integral part of the home itself. The strict border between inside and outside was eroded by the use of sheet glazing and sliding glass walls, which enabled seamless transitions between interior and exterior spaces.

Pages 158–59 The Kaufmann Desert House, Palm Springs, USA, designed by Richard Neutra.

Opposite At the Bush House in Brookfield, Queensland, Australia, Bloc Design enriched and enlivened this indoor bathing area by means of enticing, direct connections with the trees and landscape outside.

The dissolution of the boundaries between inside and out rapidly became one of the liberating glories of the modern home .... It gave rise to the idea of the 'outdoor room': an easily accessible haven that could be treated as an additional seating or dining area, with the benefit of being out in the fresh air.

Above An integrated terrace at the recently restored Garcia House in Los Angeles, CA (1962), by John Lautner, offers a wonderful vantage point and connects gently and easily with interior living spaces.

Opposite Timber decks and sun loungers at Cheong Yew Kuan's home in Ubud, Bali, project outwards into the lush greenery, while verandas and a swimming pool are a few steps away.

One sees this, especially, in many of the pioneering California Modernist homes of the 1940s, 1950s and 1960s, where this borderland was so successfully blurred, making the most of the benign climate. Richard Neutra's Kaufmann House features retractable glass walls, which promote a sense of free movement between the main living area and terraces, pool area and gardens alongside. John Lautner's futuristic Elrod House (1968), also in Palm Springs, balances the heavy mass of concrete construction with great expanses of glazing opening up to the desert landscape, while a curved glass wall retracts at the touch of a button, opening up to the terrace and kidney-shaped swimming pool.

In France in a slightly earlier period, Le Corbusier included a large elevated roof terrace and sundeck on the upper levels of his iconic Villa Savoye (1931). These terraces feature integrated planters, but the uppermost sundeck also offers a viewing platform to appreciate the gardens and surroundings.

These are buildings that stepped away from the Georgian and Victorian idea that a house should dominate the landscape or impose itself upon it. Instead, they sought connection with their surroundings rather like a belvedere. They were platforms for appreciating nature and the open skies, looking outwards rather than inwards.

The dissolution of the boundaries between inside and out rapidly became one of the liberating glories of the modern home. It allowed an easy progression from indoors to outdoors, with terraces, decks and gardens seen as extensions of living space rather than as completely separate from the home. It gave rise to the idea of the 'outdoor room': an easily accessible haven that could be treated as an additional seating or dining area, with the benefit of being out in the fresh air. The outdoor room has now become a familiar and desirable concept, especially for the new natural home.

Outdoor Rooms

The outdoor room takes many forms, of course. Some see it primarily as a veranda or porch: a man-made, semi-sheltered area from which you can appreciate nature, a garden and your surroundings. In this connection, houses such as John Friedman and Alice Kimm's King Residence in Santa Monica, California (see page 96) have taken the idea of the traditional front porch and reinvented it in a very contemporary manner, complemented by pools and drought-resistant planting.

For many of us, our garden room takes the form of a landscaped terrace or deck, easily accessed from our key living spaces. This is a place for relaxing, dining and entertaining with that easy sense of connection both to the inside of the home and the garden. It is a halfway point, softened with planters and vines perhaps, with some source of shade to offer protection from the sun at the hottest times of the day.

Outdoor rooms seek to dissolve boundaries not only between inside and out but also between house and garden, the artificial and the natural. They foster that sense of connection with nature, with the cycle of the seasons, and provide a viewing point from which to appreciate plantings and the subtle day-to-day routines of birds and wildlife.

Green Spaces

But it is the garden itself that offers key environmental benefits which enhance the pleasures of the new natural home. A garden may take many forms, from a traditional planted area to a container garden sitting on a terrace, or a roof garden, or even a 'vertical garden' – a green screen to soften the outline of a home and provide a welcome element of foliage. Green roofs –

composed of a series of layers including a waterproof membrane, a drainage layer, a filter mat, a growing medium and the planting itself – similarly help to minimize the impact of a building on the landscape while offering many of the benefits of any more traditional garden.

A garden – however modest – is a living ecosystem, providing a habitat for all kinds of wildlife, from insects to birds and beyond. Plants and trees act as a natural carbon soak, drawing in carbon dioxide and giving out oxygen, as they use CO_2 in the process of photosynthesis to make sugars to help plants grow and develop. So any garden helps in the process of oxygenating the atmosphere and reducing CO_2, the principal greenhouse gas influencing climate change. When the garden also includes significant shrubs and trees, naturally the impact is improved.

More than this, gardens and green spaces help to prevent problems such as flash flooding, an increasing issue in urban areas where so many gardens have been paved over, making it difficult for water to soak away into the ground naturally.

At the same time, of course, any garden is a place of natural beauty that promotes a sense of well-being. Planting a garden in some ways helps us give back to the environment – by offsetting the energy and carbon emissions created in the construction of the house – as well as being a joy in itself.

Planting choices, meanwhile, have been dominated by more common-sense approaches that maximize the use of indigenous and regional species, rather than non-indigenous selections that may require more maintenance and watering, as well as being vulnerable to the local climate. Increasingly, attention is being paid to the suitability of plants for regional climates, with drought-tolerant and low water-drawing plants chosen for areas of little rainfall. At the same time, a naturalistic approach to planting design is becoming increasingly prevalent, with a wider use of grasses, meadow flowers, shrubs and trees to create a more varied and rugged habitat for wildlife than a manicured garden might offer.

At the same time, gardens have a role to play in the everyday pattern of consumption within a household. Routine use of composting bins helps radically to reduce the amount of waste in refuse-collection systems, as well as providing a valuable source of enriched mulch and fertilizer.

Water recycling and storage systems for areas of low rainfall can also be integrated into the design of home and garden and used for watering plants, as well as offering a potential source of greywater for flushing toilets, along with sourcing water features. Pools, meanwhile, can offer help in naturally cooling terraces and indoor/outdoor spaces as they benefit from an evaporative effect on hot days – a traditional idea in many parts of the world that has been reinvented within modern homes and gardens.

Sky Gardens

Within more constrained urban sites, natural light, outdoor living spaces and modest gardens are priorities; this has led to increasingly inventive design solutions. Within the city, courtyard houses have become one popular way of dealing with such issues while also retaining privacy. Principal rooms look onto a courtyard garden that provides valuable outdoor space while doubling as a light well, as seen in the elevated courtyard designed by James Russell for his family home in Brisbane, Australia (see page 80), complete with green lawn.

At the same time, many architects and designers are also looking at the idea of roof terraces and sky gardens – both private

Above Trees frame a view into the bedroom pavilion at Cheong Yew Kuan's home in Bali, with a fluid crossover between indoors and outdoors.

Opposite A retractable roof on the top floor of the Elliott House in Highgate, London, by architects Eldridge Smerin, allows the kitchen and dining area to enjoy a close relationship with the sky and towering trees, while also helping to cool the house naturally in summer.

A garden – however modest – is a living ecosystem, providing a habitat for all kinds of wildlife, from insects to birds and beyond.

Above This green wall alongside the garden terrace of the Henning/Wansbrough Residence in Sydney, Australia, designed by architect Steve Kennedy, is also a treatment plant for recycling greywater so that it can be used to flush toilets or run the washing machine.

and communal – that make more of the underused resource of the urban roof line. There is increasing experimentation with the idea of substantial sky gardens integrated within and on top of new buildings, as architects, engineers and landscape designers have found ways to deal with the significant additional weight of soil and planting involved while also using new-generation membranes that protect spaces within the building from water penetration. Such gardens are becoming increasingly sophisticated and ambitious, with the inclusion not just of grasses and low-maintenance planting but also of shrubs and smaller species of trees.

This is not to say that more familiar roof terraces are not a valuable resource as well. Even modestly sized spaces are being treated in imaginative ways, providing vital outdoor areas for summer living and entertaining. Planters with bamboo, bay or climbers can form living screens to provide shade and privacy in an urban context. Vertical climbing gardens also offer a source of greenery where space is limited or there is a real benefit in softening the outline of a building, as seen at the Bricault House in Los Angeles (see page 214).

In Sebastian Mariscal's Wabi House (see page 54), a roof garden on the upper level adds to the pools, planting and rear garden at ground level. This elevated garden sits alongside the master bedroom, offering additional exterior space as well as a soft line of greenery that connects with the hillside tree lines in the distance.

There is little doubt that sky gardens of all kinds will become a progressively more important part of the urban roofscape, offering amenity space, beauty and modest but vital habitats that will benefit the natural diversity of our cities. The garden, in a multitude of forms, will always have a significant role in the evolution of the new natural home.

SUMMARY

General

* Consider the provision of outdoor space from the very beginning of any design and planning process. Think of interior and exterior space as two parts of a whole rather than completely separate entities.
* Where space is tight, look at designs that may offer outdoor spaces with minimal impact on the footprint of the house. These might include roof terraces or courtyard gardens, which can double as light wells.
* Communal green space is also a valuable resource, so bear in mind easy access to parks, allotments and other amenity spaces when selecting a site or building.
* Factor in any ground works early on that might affect landscaping. Projects such as installing rainwater-harvesting storage tanks, wells, pipework and coils or boreholes for ground-water heat pumps can involve considerable upheaval.
* Respect existing planting or trees on the site and be prepared to replace greenery that might be lost or damaged during building or landscaping works.
* Take into account the potential maintenance involved when creating gardens and outdoor spaces. If a low-maintenance approach is needed, research materials and plant choices that require low levels of ongoing care, along with ideas such as protective membranes and bark mulches that may help prevent weeds developing.
* Provide for everyday routines such as composting within the design and layout of a garden or outdoor space. Home composting bins cut down hugely on waste that may need collection, as well as providing free fertilizer.
* In areas of low rainfall, look into rainwater harvesting and provision of rainwater storage, which at its simplest might take the form of water barrels. This can prove a valuable resource for watering gardens in the drier months.

Dissolving Boundaries

* As well as introducing natural light, the use of considerable banks of glazing and sliding glass doors and walls will promote a sense of connection with exterior space and help to 'frame' key vistas and views.
* When positioning windows and openings, take into account not only practical issues such as the provision of light and privacy but also aesthetic or poetic considerations to do with the desire to capture and appreciate particular portions of the landscape from within the home.
* Ensure easy access to outdoor rooms and terraces. Spaces used for outdoor eating and entertaining, for instance, will usually need to be within easy reach of the kitchen.
* Consider issues of privacy and security when designing areas of easy flow from interior to exterior space. Avoid overlooking neighbours' gardens and outdoor areas, and ensure that all windows and doors can be properly secured when not in use.

Outdoor Living

* Consider, ideally, the provision of contrasting outdoor rooms, perhaps one that is more open for daytime use and something more protected and intimate for evenings and entertaining.
* Look into the need for shading when positioning an outdoor room (see Chapter 2). Shading might ideally be provided by tree cover or planting; alternatively, awnings and canopies may be required.
* Carefully relate outdoor rooms both to the architecture and design of the house itself and to the planning and orientation of the garden or other exterior space.
* Pools or water features may help to enhance an outdoor room, preferably fed by harvested rainwater, as well as providing a naturally cooling evaporative effect on hot days.
* Make sure that outdoor furniture is hard-wearing, robust and low-maintenance. If necessary, be prepared to store it over the winter months or during extreme weather to avoid damage and ensure a long, useful life.
* Provide adequate garden or garage storage for family detritus. As with the interiors of the home, storage is always a necessity.

Planting

* Consider planting schemes within the context of minimizing the impact of the building on the environment. This might involve the use of green screens, roof gardens, hedging and green roofs.
* Look at planting as a way of enhancing your privacy, especially in urban areas where 'walls' of bamboo, grasses, shrubs, small trees or climbers might be an alternative to solid and artificial boundaries. But respect your neighbours' right to light and ensure that such boundaries are not allowed to get out of hand.
* Remember to compare the benefits of evergreen and deciduous planting. If planting is used to provide privacy, for instance, then evergreen plants or trees would be advisable.
* Use indigenous or hardy plants suited to the local climate. High-maintenance and vulnerable planting should be used sparingly or knowledgeably.
* In areas at risk of low rainfall or drought, research drought-resistant planting and avoid planting that may require constant watering.
* Given the countless benefits of home-grown and organic produce, look at incorporating fruit trees, herbs and vegetable beds into your garden design where possible. In restricted spaces, containers can be used to grow your own herbs and vegetables.
* Keep in mind the suitability of plant choices for areas of shade, partial shade and full sunlight. Always seek advice if you are not sure of the suitability of plants for certain parts of your garden.
* For larger gardens, consider devoting parts to more naturalistic and rugged planting, such as meadow grasses and flowers or copses, which may offer a more varied habitat for wildlife as well as aesthetic interest.
* For terraces, roof gardens, courtyards and more restricted areas, planters and containers can be used to powerful effect. Seek advice on plants that may thrive all the better within limited root space.

Roof Gardens

* Roof terraces and sky gardens can become seductive vantage points from which to appreciate the landscape and surroundings, as well as providing outdoor space for buildings with limited opportunities for other kinds of exterior spaces.
* Take care with issues of weight and loading. The engineering of the roof must allow for the additional weight of people and planting, as well as the very considerable weight of any soil and other materials.
* Heavy-duty and specialist membranes will be needed for roof gardens exposed to wear and tear. This is especially true of sky gardens and green roofs where planting is placed directly upon the roof itself. Such membranes, of course, need to be long-lasting and watertight.
* Keep issues of access in mind. Like any garden, terraces and roof gardens need regular care and maintenance so materials and waste need to be easily taken up and down.
* Ensure that roof gardens are very well secured with balustrades and railings, especially if they might be used by families with young children.

Green Roofs

* Always use well-trained specialist engineers and contractors when creating a green roof. Errors with waterproof membranes or loading could compromise the structural integrity of a building.
* Green roofs can provide good insulation for a home – helping to improve the overall thermal performance of a building – as well as contributing to a reduction in air pollution and runoff, while also promoting biodiversity.
* Green roofs often come in the form of ready-formed plant 'blankets', frequently made of sedum. Other green roofs are planted with grasses.
* Planted roofs can make a significant visual impact and help soften the appearance of a building.
* A green roof – like any roof – will need maintenance, careful monitoring and possible watering in sustained periods of dry weather.

This house possesses an extraordinary synergy with its seductive surroundings: it is a platform for viewing and appreciating nature.

HOUSE IN IPORANGA, GUARUJA, BRAZIL

STUDIO ARTHUR CASAS

'I have always wanted a house in the middle of the forest,' says architect Arthur Casas, 'a place where I can recharge my energy.' Casas has certainly achieved that within this enticing retreat in the Atlantic rainforest, around two hours' drive from São Paulo and a short distance from the sea.

This house possesses an extraordinary synergy with its seductive surroundings: it is a platform for viewing and appreciating nature. The double-height central section opens up completely, through a vast assembly of sliding glass walls, to create a powerful feeling of transparency that allows the landscape to feed into and pass through the heart of the building. The borders between indoor space and exterior terraces dissolve, creating a serene and contemplative haven.

'I wanted a neutral space not only to balance the brilliance of the rainforest but also because I wanted a place to switch off,' says Casas, who shares the house with his wife Marai Valente and their young daughter. 'We live a simpler life here.'

The design and construction of the house pay absolute respect to the beauty of the natural context. Casas was careful not to remove any trees from the site, allowing the forest to form the verdant backdrop to the building. Interior and exterior finishes are tied together with one another and the surrounding forest by the use of Brazilian camaru – a strong native teak from sustainable sources – which can withstand the effects of the tropical heat.

The central living space gives way to terraces with built-in provision for outdoor dining and relaxing and with easy access to the kitchen and utility spaces inside. The central section of the house is open-plan and 35 feet (10.5 metres) high, with a bridge spanning the void to connect the bedrooms on the upper level of the two distinct wings. The visual impact of this bridge is softened by the use of glass balustrades, so it does not interfere with the sense of transparency, while the stairway to one side of the central sitting room was also designed with the lightest of touches and made with cantilevered timber steps emerging from a side wall.

On the lower level, utility spaces and the kitchen are positioned within one wing and a guest bedroom and a studio in the other. The desk in the studio is positioned in front of a window, looking out into the landscape, while a large glass side door allows ready access to the terrace, a natural extension of the internal living space. The terraces feature elements such as built-in furniture, pool, outdoor shower and integrated Japanese-style barbecue next to the outside dining table. 'Every element is designed to embrace the surroundings,' says Casas.

Pages 168–71 Vast and retractable glass walls pull away to either side of the house to allow a full sense of transparency and an openness to the verdant jungle greenery that surrounds the building. The double-height central living room is spanned by a lightly conceived bridge with glass balustrades, connecting bedrooms at either end of the upper level.

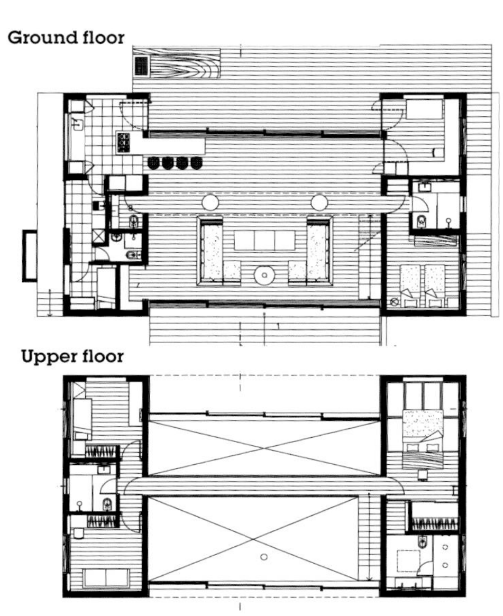

Opposite and above The through-flow from interior to exterior space is easy and seamless, with a series of choices created between indoor and outdoor living. With the glass walls open, the house becomes a pavilion or belvedere. 'We wanted a place for interaction not only with our living spaces but with the surroundings,' says Casas.

Above and opposite Exterior spaces become a delightful series of outdoor rooms, with tailored areas for dining and sitting out. The exterior dining table is a bespoke piece by Casas, incorporating a Japanese-style hibachi grill. The use of camaru wood for cladding and decks, as well as interior elements, helps unify the house and tie the spaces together.

This is a highly flexible house that can also protect itself against more extreme winter conditions while providing retreats and intimate spaces, as well as open summer living.

PALM BEACH HOUSE, PALM BEACH, SYDNEY, NSW, AUSTRALIA

DESIGN KING COMPANY

Making the most of an extraordinary view of the Pacific, the Palm Beach House is as much a belvedere as a practical but beautiful family home. Pushed into a hillside overlooking the ocean, the house opens up to the vista and draws it indoors through a deft and dynamic use of retractable glass walls. At the same time, this is a highly flexible house that can also protect itself against more extreme winter conditions while providing retreats and intimate spaces, as well as open summer living.

'Everything about the site pushed us in the direction of diffusing the boundary between inside and outside,' says architect Jon King. 'But while it's clear that Sydney has a kind climate, there are times when a house must be closed up and become protective in nature.'

The extraordinary site was bought at auction by Pat and Bill Rice, who wanted to create a vacation and weekend home for themselves and their four children. At the same time they wanted the option of moving into the house full-time at some point. The entry, to the rear, opens up to key living spaces on the main level, which also holds the family bedrooms. Guest accommodation, utility spaces, a home theatre and a darkroom are all positioned on a more recessive lower level. Interiors were designed in collaboration with designer Stephen Collins.

The layout is fluid, with a large central sitting room opening out to a terrace and outdoor seating area via a sliding wall of glass. To one side of the sitting room sit the kitchen and dining room. Here the glass walls fold away completely, allowing a powerful sense of connection with the outdoors and views of the ocean. This is reinforced by the use of a protective glass balustrade on the adjoining terrace, which provides safety but also an unimpeded view from the dining table. Tracked diaphanous curtains provide shade when needed, while the overhanging eaves help to protect the interiors against the heat of the midday sun.

The principal bedrooms are situated to the other side of the central sitting room. The master bedroom and bathroom are enriched with a small internal courtyard garden that pushes its way into the outline of the house, providing extra light and a further sense of connection to the outdoors, as well as additional cross-ventilation.

Existing angophora trees – similar to eucalyptus – were preserved and native bushland around the house regenerated. Additional planting in the entrance courtyard and around the building is indigenous and sympathetic while tying in with the use of natural materials and textures in the house itself, including timber and stone.

Ground floor

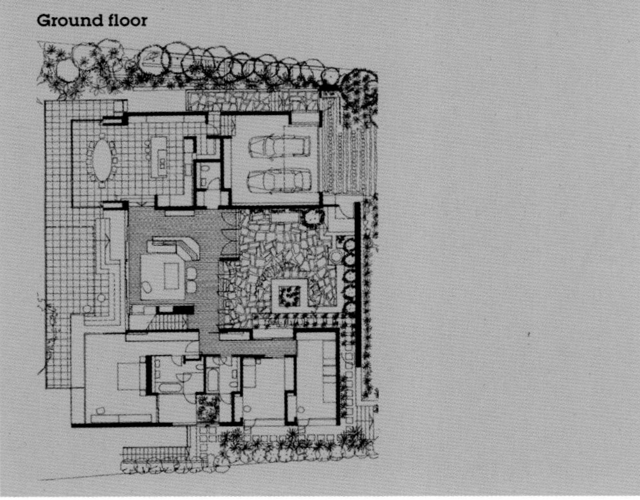

Pages 176–81 A key aspect of the design of the house is the way it feels at its best in very different seasons and conditions. This is partly achieved by means of glass doors that can fold or retract, allowing light and air to pass through. Clerestory windows at ceiling height in the central living room also encourage a rich quality of natural light. Planting and established eucalyptus trees provide a natural brise soleil.

Opposite and this page The highly flexible, adaptable and fluid design of the house allows it to open up dramatically in the summer months, making the most of the ocean views and achieving simple transitions between indoor and outdoor living. 'Not many houses have that sense of elevation, where the ocean really becomes part of the house,' says architect Jon King. In the summer, diaphanous curtains and drapes are used to help provide shade when needed for the dining area. The overhang of the roof also softens the impact of the sun.

'The natural scenery of the Luberon is such a marvel, we had to question what it would accept and absorb without breaking the subtle harmony that exists between vegetation, stones and buildings.'

HOUSE G, LUBERON, FRANCE

STUDIO KO

Nestled in the rugged landscape of the Luberon in southern France, House G is the soul of discretion. With its green, planted roof and protective walls made of local stone, the low-slung house almost disappears into the land, making only the lightest of impressions upon the countryside.

For owner Thierry Gautier and his architects – Karl Fournier and Olivier Marty of Studio KO – the key aspect of the design was to celebrate the views out across the landscape, opening the house up to the extraordinary vista. 'We had the idea of designing the house as a "camera obscura" aimed at the landscape,' says Fournier. 'So we have walls to the sides and openings at the two ends.'

Gautier, who is a director at the jewelry company Van Cleef & Arpels, had known the area for many years, having first come across it during a holiday. He later bought a farm there, which he restored. But he then decided that he wanted to build a house from scratch and found a suitable piece of land not far from a small village.

Gautier had known of Studio KO for some time, as the architects had done work for Van Cleef & Arpels. Gautier was particularly impressed by a number of houses they had designed in Morocco, evidence of a special sensitivity to landscape and the use of local materials and building techniques. House G also adopts an understanding of context and tradition while at the same time creating an atmosphere that is original, contemporary and rich in character.

Working in conjunction with local architect Michel Escande, Studio KO took some time to obtain planning permission to build in an area of such natural beauty. But the planning authorities were reassured by the way in which the design of the building sought to caress rather than dominate the landscape.

'Integrating the house with the landscape was part of the brief,' says Gautier. 'We didn't want a high building but to work with very simple lines. The idea was that we could float inside the space and that the view would be the real masterpiece.'

The upper level of the house, then, holds all the main living spaces, culminating in an open-plan kitchen, dining and living area with large pivoting windows that overlook the swimming pool and terrace below. Bedrooms and service spaces are pushed to the rear and a subservient lower floor. In addition to the use of local stone and the green roof, the house is naturally ventilated and fed by electricity from a local hydro-electric station.

'It was important to us to have a sense of responsibility to the landscape,' says Fournier. 'The natural scenery of the Luberon is such a marvel, we had to question what it would accept and absorb without breaking the subtle harmony that exists between vegetation, stones and buildings.'

Pages 184–87 With its green roof and protective outer walls made of local stone, the house effectively disappears into the undulating landscape. This is a structure that celebrates and respects the countryside, using simple lines and forms – also seen in the low-slung pool area and terracing – to soften the visual impact.

Pages 188–91 Placing the main living spaces on the upper storey created a powerful vantage point looking out across the pool. The interiors are purposefully restrained so that the emphasis is on the natural setting. 'We wanted to magnify the view by using the furniture in quite a minimalist way,' says Gautier. 'The important thing about designing a house like this is that it feels timeless,' adds Fournier.

The house is a kind of pergola integrated into the greenery of the carefully preserved site. Vines grow over a trellis at the front of house, offering shade but also allowing the house to melt into the countryside.

MAISON OLLIOULES, VAR, FRANCE

RUDY RICCIOTTI ARCHITECTE

Looking out from the hills of the Var towards the Mediterranean, Maison Ollioules has the feeling of a belvedere. Tucked into the landscape and largely on a single level, this is a modest but beautiful pavilion that opens itself up to the vista and fits into the restored terraces and ancient stone walls around the building.

But at the same time, the house is a kind of pergola integrated into the greenery of the carefully preserved site. Vines grow over a trellis at the front of the house, offering shade but also allowing the house to disappear into the countryside, while a planted green roof enhances the concept of natural camouflage.

'We wanted the house to melt into the landscape, respecting nature, and to have a discreet rapport with the neighbourhood,' says Eliane Cleenewerck, who commissioned the house with her husband, Jean-Louis. 'The most important things for us, as well as the space itself, were the discretion of the construction and the fact that the house should not spoil the terrain, while caring for the trees. We also wanted a house on one level and that feeling of being outside even when we are inside.'

The Cleenewercks, who run a business consultancy, decided to move to the South of France from Paris and searched for a suitable spot to build a house for some time. Eventually they found their hillside site, not far from Toulon, and asked architect Rudy Ricciotti if he would design a house for them. Ricciotti is based in the South of France, understands the area well, and has designed a number of contemporary houses in the region with particular sensitivity to the landscape, as well as a strong sense of connection to their surroundings.

The Cleenewercks had known of Ricciotti's work for some time and the architect visited the site, talked with his clients and by the end of the same day had come up with some preliminary designs for the house that were carried through to the finished building.

The house is dominated by a large, open-plan living, dining and kitchen area flowing out onto the terraces. Bedrooms and other ancillary spaces are positioned at the opposite end of the house, with a more intimate and enclosed evening sitting room positioned in a sunken basement.

Material choices – largely concrete and glass – are kept simple and the furniture is minimal. Again, this maximizes the importance of the view, while elements such as an internal cactus garden, the terracing and the pool area all reinforce the importance of the inside/outside relationship.

'If country houses really blended with the countryside, like our own house, then there would be more of a sense of connection between nature and home,' says Eliane Cleenewerck. 'We love everything about the house, but especially the constant sense of light and having the panoramic view. The house is truly a belvedere.'

Ground floor

Pages 192–95 The discreetly positioned house explores ideas of natural camouflage to soften its impression on the landscape. The house effectively fits onto a shallow step on the hillside and hides itself with its green roof and a canopy of vines and climbers that forms a sun screen at the front. It is a home that is as much about outside space as indoor living, with particular importance given to the terracing, decks and pool area.

This page and opposite
Planting around the house – as well as a cactus garden in the bedroom – softens its rectangular lines. Even from within spaces such as the bedroom or living room, the focal point is the dramatic view offered by the hillside positioning of the structure. Retractable glass doors in the main living area dissolve the boundaries between inside and out, while awnings over the dining area on the terrace complement the natural shade provided by the vines and climbers.

'Because of the mild climate the garden is considered as much a living space as the interior. We design to embrace the climate and this is done for environmental reasons, but is also a fundamental part of the lifestyle, especially for a house so close to the beach.'

WAVE HOUSE, SYDNEY, NSW, AUSTRALIA

TONY OWEN PARTNERS

Designed for a supplier of architectural glass and his family, the Wave House in Bondi Beach makes best use of sliding glass walls and a mix of windows to create a strong sense of connection to its rear garden while introducing a wealth of natural light. It is also a dynamic building that explores a series of intriguing contrasts between openness and enclosure, the transparent and the opaque, sinuous curves and crisp geometry.

The front of the house is largely closed to the nearby street, with a parking area and a series of more enclosed spaces – such as a playroom and study – acting as a buffer between the entry area and the main living spaces to the rear. Here the house opens up in dramatic fashion, with a large open-plan living, dining and kitchen area leading to a retractable wall of glass, which pushes right back to create a seamless transition out onto the terrace and into the modest rear garden.

'In Australia these days the design of houses starts with examining the relationship between inside and outside,' says architect Tony Owen, who worked on the project in collaboration with Pearl Todd Interiors and landscape architect Volker Klem. 'Because of the mild climate the garden is considered as much a living space as the interior. We design to embrace the climate and this is done for environmental reasons, but is also a fundamental part of the lifestyle, especially for a house so close to the beach.'

Additional banks of glazing to one side of the living room and alongside the kitchen allow a clear sense of connection to the garden, with its simple but effective planting scheme complemented by a pond. With additional panels of glazing – translucent and opaque – at ceiling height, the quality of natural light is impressive, while the openness of the building allows for natural cross-ventilation.

The concrete floor pad, with its high thermal mass, helps to regulate the temperature of the house, while a solar-gain strategy is also used to help warm the building naturally in winter. All glazing is of high-specification low-emissivity glass.

On the upper level, the master bedroom to the rear also benefits from a bank of glazing leading out to an elevated terrace overlooking the garden below. The dynamic quality of the house is reinforced by the repetition of the idea of this sinuous structural wave carrying through the form of the building, with its flowing ceilings and roof line cresting within the rear spaces and echoed in – for instance – the sculpted form of the concrete island in the kitchen.

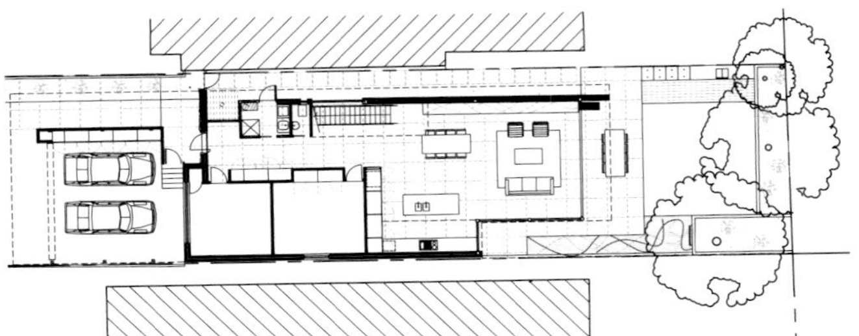

Ground floor

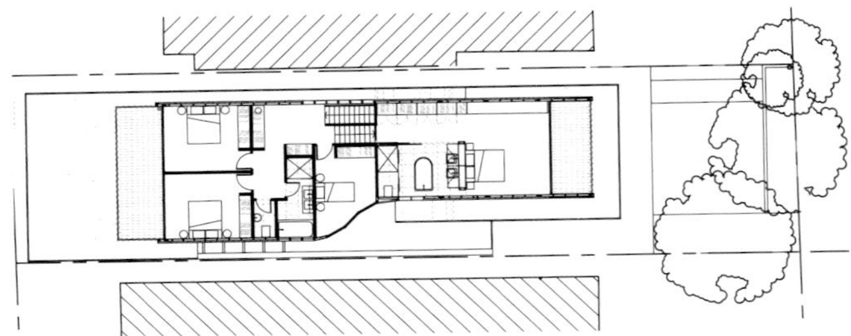

Upper floor

Pages 198–201 While more enclosed to the front, where the house meets the neighbouring street, the Wave House opens up in dramatic fashion to the rear, where the interiors unfold and embrace the gardens. A sliding glass wall between the main, open-plan living area and the rear terrace and garden allows indoor and outdoor zones to blend. An additional band of glazing towards the ceiling of this area brings in more sunlight; the house uses solar gain in winter and natural ventilation in summer to reduce running costs.

Opposite and this page The quality of openness and light adds to the luxurious quality of the house, yet here luxury is defined more in terms of a richness of space while the approach to the interiors is generally minimalist. Many different glazing elements and types – from slot windows to translucent panels to frosted shower enclosures – are used to transmit and circulate light throughout. The fluid form of the wave motif in the ceiling, kitchen island and stairway adds to the dynamic character of the house.

5| sustainable footprints

sustainable footprints

Just over 10 per cent of all global greenhouse-gas emissions come from heating, cooling and powering our homes, according to a recent report by the World Resources Institute. That is around the same percentage as total emissions from road transport, while – just for comparison – air travel is responsible for under 2 per cent of global greenhouse-gas emissions. This is without even taking into account the emissions of CO_2 involved in manufacturing construction materials – such as cement, steel and aluminium – to build our homes in the first place.

This makes our houses among the most significant contributors to climate change on the planet. It's not difficult to project some years into the future towards a time when the idea of burning valuable resources like oil and gas just to keep the air conditioning running will seem quite ridiculous, as well as destructive.

When you look at these kinds of figures it is no wonder that so much attention has been, and should be, devoted to greener ways of providing home energy. While the subject comes last in this book, it is worth repeating that green energy can only be one part of the creation of a sustainable new natural home.

The design and build of a house – while creating a welcoming, beautiful environment for ourselves and our families – has to take into account the essential task of reducing the amount of energy we need to power our homes in the first place. As we have seen, this means paying close attention to basic strategies such as high-spec insulation, which will help our homes retain heat in cooler months while regulating temperatures in warmer months, while solar gain should be used to help warm them.

Reducing energy consumption through design also means using natural ventilation techniques – such as cross-ventilation and the venting of hot air via skylights – that do away with the need for air-conditioning units. Maximizing natural light through glazing, skylights and other features such as light wells also leads to less energy spent on artificial lighting. Close attention paid to the use of more eco-friendly construction materials can also help to minimize the impact of our homes on the environment and the embodied energy within them.

Reducing the amount of energy we use in our homes, then, has to go hand-in-hand with the production of greener forms of energy. The less energy we use, the less we need to produce in the first place and the more minimal the impact on greenhouse-gas emissions and climate change. The use of 'smart' meters and monitors can assist in regulating the amount of power used in our homes and make us more aware of the daily ebb and flow of energy.

The new natural home aims to minimize its impact on the environment in every sense, from energy use to choice of materials, from landscaping and green roofs to home composting. It means adopting a different mindset and – as architect Glenn Murcutt has put it – touching the earth a little more lightly.

Burning Money

While the need to reduce home carbon emissions to fight climate change is a key priority, the other major imperative driving us to cut down on energy is, of course, money. With the rising cost of energy – particularly of the tanks of oil and gas needed to heat many country homes – few of us can afford to ignore the warning signs. Energy bills will continue to rise for the foreseeable future as global demand gradually increases, which will push us into reducing power consumption in whatever ways we can, but also encourage the search for alternative sources of energy.

The good news is that we are seeing a significant amount of research and investment into numerous different kinds of green and renewable energy. In many developed countries, there is a push to construct new wind farms – both onshore and offshore – as well as biomass plants, hydro-electric plants and, much more controversially, nuclear power facilities. At the same time we are seeing more research into solar power stations and wave-energy installations.

Depending on the site and situation of an individual building, some home energy solutions will be more appropriate than others, and some may be of little value and could never really pay back the initial installation investment.

Pages 204–5 The Simpson-Lee House, New South Wales, Australia by Glenn Murcutt.

Page 206 A view across the deck at garden designer Rick Eckersley's holiday home on Mornington Peninsula in Australia shows the windmill used to pump water to a natural swimming pond and wetland dam.

Above and opposite At the Tinbeerwah House in Noosa, Australia, by Bark Design, large water-storage tanks collect rainwater from the roof while a concrete plunge pool offers compact summertime heat relief.

But all of this new infrastructure will take time and massive investment, which means higher energy bills. Add this to the costs of oil, gas and coal used in older power stations, and it is clear that we are decades away from energy that is both clean and easily affordable.

This has led to an encouraging push into energy micro-generation, either at community level or for individual homes. In the mountain village of Lech in Austria, for example, a communal biomass plant was built to provide piped hot water for homes and other buildings (see page 246). The biomass plant is fed using offcuts and waste from the local forestry industry, which is managed on sustainable principles. Many other biomass plants have been developed in the region, providing a degree of energy independence and reducing the need to transmit or transport energy over long distances.

This is an example of win-win living. Trees capture carbon and release oxygen as they grow, the timber is used in construction once harvested, and the waste byproduct goes into the biomass plant to generate energy. Little wonder that biomass is one of the great hopes of the green power industry, with the prospect of additional forestry and short-rotation coppicing brought into use to help power biomass plants, as well as burning organic waste as fuel rather than sending it to landfill.

In the absence of such communal projects, homeowners are increasingly looking at ways of generating their own energy and getting themselves – as far as possible – off the grid.

Off the Grid

There has been a temptation to rush into home power generation in the hope of a quick-fix solution to reducing energy bills and playing a part in helping reduce carbon emissions. However laudable the motives, though, micro-generation is not something that should be rushed into without looking at other energy-saving measures and ideas.

Depending on the site and situation of an individual building, some home energy solutions will be more appropriate than others, and some may be of little value and could never really pay back the initial installation investment. Adding a mini-wind turbine to the roof of an urban or suburban home, for instance, may have only the most minor of benefits unless the technology improves in coming years.

Given the many different kinds of systems available, it is a subject that should be carefully researched and discussed with an architect or consultant, bearing in mind the specific conditions that apply to your site or home. It has become clear, though, that some home energy sources do have considerable advantages and can clearly pay for themselves over the long term.

Biomass Boilers

While community biomass projects of the kind developed in Lech and other parts of the world have great potential, an alternative option is to install a home biomass boiler. Such boilers run on the same principles as standard oil- or gas-fired boilers, providing hot water for heating and from the tap. They are fed either by woodchip or – more commonly – by timber pellets made of compressed sawdust, which are tidier and take up less space. Given that considerable quantities of either are needed to keep such boilers running, storage will be needed either alongside or nearby. Biomass boilers can be fed with an automated system or manually. Manual feeding – which means a bag full of pellets at a time – requires someone to be around, of course, and is a commitment. Ash also needs to be removed regularly – usually every few months from more sophisticated systems.

Given that storage space is required, biomass boilers are especially suited to country homes, where the boiler can be positioned in its own power room, shed or cellar with an adjoining fuel store. Care is needed to make sure that fuel is sourced from approved suppliers using sustainably managed forestry and should also be sourced locally or regionally.

Wood-burning stoves and even standard fires are also a form of biomass and can, of course, help heat a particular room or rooms. For a thermally efficient home with high standards of insulation, the benefits can spread much further. It is also a system that can be relatively easily retrofitted to existing or period houses, as long as space is available for the stove itself and for storage.

Ground-source Heat Pumps

Drawing readily available energy from the ground sounds like another win-win situation, so it is no wonder that ground-source heat pumps have become increasingly popular with architects and homeowners in recent years.

Ground-source heat pumps rely on a system of submerged pipes buried in the ground, either via a borehole on limited sites or through a system of coils in trenches under a garden or outdoor space. Liquid (usually a brine solution) is pumped through this closed loop of submerged pipes, gently warmed by the higher temperatures to be found beneath the ground. A heat-pump unit in the home then concentrates this heat as it passes through, until it reaches a temperature high enough to be used to help heat the house, usually via underfloor heating. A hot-water thermal store can be used to increase the efficiency of the system.

'If you talk to most mechanical and electrical consultants working on sustainable houses then you will find that there is a whole menu of different technologies that you can use,' says British architect James Gorst, designer of Glen View in Suffolk (see page 224). 'But only a few of them are economically pragmatic and really make sense. There's no doubt in my mind that ground-source heat pumps do work and provide constant heating at an economically advantageous rate.'

A geo-technical survey of a site will be needed to ensure that the system will deliver enough capacity to make the investment worthwhile. Installing the system will cause upheaval inside and outside the home, so needs to be well integrated into the building and landscaping process. Such systems are not generally suitable for providing domestic hot water. Some statistics suggest a considerable saving on carbon emissions and a payback period of around fifteen years. The whole process can be run in reverse in hotter periods to cool the home.

Solar Panels

Solar panels are another flexible system that can be retrofitted to existing buildings or integrated into a new-build scheme. Unsurprisingly, they are at their most effective in areas of readily available sunlight, not so good in poor light levels.

Essentially solar panels come in two different forms: photovoltaics (PV), for producing electricity from the power of the sun, and solar thermal, which turns energy from the sun into hot water, usually for domestic use from the tap but sometimes for heating.

PV technology has improved greatly in recent years and is used in an increasingly wide range of applications, including helping to power homes. When sunshine hits a PV cell it generates electricity, which can be used as an alternative to power from the grid.

Solar panels are usually positioned on the roof, placed to take best advantage of the movement of the sun (usually facing south in the northern hemisphere and the opposite way in the southern hemisphere). Solar electric roof tiles are also an option for a more discreet look to the roof line, although they can be more expensive than PV panels. Excess electricity can sometimes be sold back to the grid.

Solar thermal systems can generate as much as two thirds of the hot-water needs of a home, depending on water use and sunlight hours. The solar collectors again come in the form of panels – in a tubular or flat-plate design – which can be fitted to the roof or sides of a building. Liquid within the tubes is heated by the sun and taken through a heat exchanger within the home, where it heats domestic water in a tank or store.

In many seasonal climates, the drawback of the solar systems is that there will naturally be less energy or hot water in the winter months, when it is most needed. But solar systems are increasingly used in combination with other forms of micro-generation, such as biomass boilers.

Planning permission may be needed for solar panels in some areas, particularly for listed buildings. Studies suggest a payback period of around ten years.

Alternative Energy

Other sources of green energy include hydro-electric power, which has occasionally been put to use to power individual homes, farmsteads or communities. Micro-hydropower plants use the gravitational power of flowing water diverted from streams, rivers or holding lakes to run turbines to generate electricity. In reality, the complexity and cost of such schemes make them rare in a domestic setting, although hydro is a long-standing generator of power on a larger scale, particularly in mountainous areas where the geography and geology are suitable.

Wind power is a great addition to the provision of renewable energy in the form of

'Sustainability is not just about building a box on a meadow with zero energy loss, but about an acceptance and love of a building.'

Page 210 At designer Andrzej Zarzycki's family weekend house in the New Forest in England, this timber-panelled bedroom is warmed by a wood-burning stove. Additional heating for the house is provided by a wood-pellet boiler.

Above A solar thermal panel provides hot water at the Henning/Wansbrough Residence in Sydney, Australia, within a beachside eco-friendly home extended and reinvented by architect Steve Kennedy.

both onshore and offshore wind farms, with many new farms under development. The benefits of individual domestic wind turbines, though, have been questioned especially when it comes to mini-turbines bolted to the roofs of houses in built-up areas.

For wind turbines to be effective they need wind, of course, so are more suited to exposed rural sites that will justify the investment by generating a reasonable amount of power. For those who find themselves in an area of suitable wind speed, some figures suggest that the considerable investment in a stand-alone turbine could repay itself in as little as five years. For isolated areas off the grid used to relying on generators, wind turbines can prove especially beneficial.

Surveys are needed to establish the suitability of a site for a turbine, planning permission may be required and foundations are needed for masts.

New Natural

The provision of green and renewable energy is just one of many aspects of creating a new natural home. Designing or adapting a home is always complex and challenging, with so many different elements to be considered, but ultimately it is hugely rewarding. The new natural ethos suggests thinking about the home in a fresh way, building in ideas that help to minimize the impact on the environment in many different respects, while also seeking connection with nature.

This is certainly true of the design of Barrie Marshall's extraordinary home on Phillip Island in Victoria, Australia (see page 230). Situated in an area of great natural beauty, positioned right by the sea, the house is pushed into the dunes and scrubland with a roof of green grass that enfolds the building. From within, the house makes the most of the panoramic views of coast and ocean; seen from without, the structure seems almost to disappear.

Few houses may take the idea of touching the earth lightly to such extremes, and most of the houses presented in this book offer a softer approach while – hopefully – inspiring others to integrate new natural ideas into the designs of their own homes.

We return, then, to the idea of inspiring change with which we began. The home, as we have seen, is a key element in the ongoing struggle to reduce carbon emissions and fight climate change, as well as a perpetual part of the built environment that has to sit side by side with nature. The more sensitive and respectful that relationship between home and nature can become, the better, and for all sorts of powerful reasons, including the fact that our houses should also be places where we relate to and connect with the beauty of the natural world on one level or another.

'Sustainability is not just about building a box on a meadow with zero energy loss, but about an acceptance and love of a building,' says Austrian architect Philip Lutz (see page 134). 'If you love it, then you will care for it. If it's just an object then it won't last so long, it won't be passed down the generations and it won't be sustainable in the long term.'

So we should never forget that the new natural home should be a beloved haven and a place of joy, as well as a functioning, practical building. A house has always been much, much more than a machine for living in. Think of it instead as a belvedere – a carefully crafted and enticing retreat that provides us with a window on the world while reminding us of its countless charms.

SUMMARY

General

* Look at using green and renewable energy alongside a push to reduce the overall amount of power consumed in the home by exploring high-spec insulation, maximizing the benefits of solar gain and using natural ventilation techniques instead of air conditioning.
* Use 'smart' meters and electricity monitors to look at the amount of power being used in the home and how you might regulate or reduce energy use.
* In colder climates, consider mechanical ventilation with heat recovery not only to provide a building with fresh, circulated air but also to recycle valuable heat back into the building.
* Check if there might be a possibility of community micro-power-generation projects before looking at home generation. Small-scale biomass plants, in particular, are increasingly being developed to benefit modest communities and some housing or mixed-use developments.
* When considering a wind turbine or solar panels, get hold of a power-predictor kit that will readily assess the benefits of either before making a large investment.
* Consult fully with your architect, surveyor and energy consultants before investing in any home power-generation system. Building, site and conditions need careful assessment before committing to such major costs.
* Look at the payback period of any micro-generation technology, i.e. the number of years over which potential savings from a green energy system as compared to a standard energy bill will mean that the system has effectively paid for itself. This will help you weigh up the financial pros and cons of investing in micro-power generation.
* Remember that different forms of micro-energy generation can be combined in the home. The green benefits of a ground-source heat pump for heating a building, for instance, could be complemented with a wind turbine or photovoltaic panels to produce electricity.
* Consider the extent to which micro-power generation systems may need maintaining or servicing at regular intervals.
* Allow for teething troubles in any new system as you get used to it and regulate it according to the way you live, as well as the design of the house itself. Ground-source heat pumps, for instance, may need some adjustment to get a building to a comfortable and constant temperature.

Biomass

* Biomass boilers offer an alternative to conventional oil- or gas-fired home boilers, providing hot water for heating and domestic use.
* Sufficient storage is needed for woodchip or – more usually – wood pellets made of compressed sawdust used to feed the boilers. This often makes biomass boilers more suited to larger or rural homes with substantial cellars or outhouses.
* Depending on the cost and sophistication of the system, biomass boilers can be fed with woodchip or pellets manually or automatically from a storage hopper. Manual feeding needs to be part of a regular routine.
* Waste ash needs to be removed from the boiler, weekly for basic systems or every few months for more sophisticated designs.
* Ensure that woodchip or pellets are sourced from eco-friendly sources and that they are sourced locally or regionally to reduce transport miles.
* Consider wood-burning stoves or make use of existing fireplaces. If the home is well insulated, these can have a significant impact.

Ground-source Heat Pumps

* Ground-source heat pumps draw on the natural warmth of the soil to help provide warmth for the home.
* Heat pumps usually rely on a closed system of looped pipework buried in the soil, either in trenches in a garden or adjoining land or – within a smaller site – in a borehole.
* Brine solution is pumped through the pipework, and, as it passes through the pipes, the liquid is warmed gently. This heat is amplified and concentrated as it passes through the heat-pump unit and then used to heat the home, usually in the form of underfloor heating.
* You will need a geotechnical survey to assess the suitability of a site for a ground-source heat pump.
* Heat pumps – like most micro-power-generation systems – require regular inspection and servicing.
* Ground-source heat pumps are not generally used to produce high temperatures, so work best in buildings that are well insulated and with low energy demands.
* The heat pump unit itself is powered by electricity. For those concerned about being as energy-independent as possible, this is a factor to keep in mind and one reason why home heat pumps are sometimes used in combination with wind turbines or PV panels.
* With some systems, twenty-four-hour operation is recommended for maximum efficiency.
* Many systems should be able to run in reverse to help provide cooling on summer days.

Solar Energy

* PVs are used to produce electricity as sunlight passes through solar cells made of layers of semi-conductive material such as silicon. Solar thermal is a different form of panel that generates hot water.
* PVs – like solar thermal panels – are usually mounted on roofs or the sides of buildings. They need to be carefully positioned to maximize energy production, usually facing south in the northern hemisphere but facing north in the southern hemisphere.
* PV roof tiles can be used as an alternative to solar panels but can be more costly.
* PVs require an 'inverter', a box that transforms electricity from the panels into suitable home energy.
* In some countries, any excess electricity can be sold back to the regional supply grid.
* Solar thermal panels, or 'collectors', are filled with water, brine or anti-freeze solutions, which heat up in the sun and are then used to heat domestic hot water in a storage tank via a heat exchanger.
* Solar thermal is used in conjunction with traditional water-heating methods – such as electricity and boilers – that kick in to provide domestic hot water at times when the power of the sun proves inadequate.
* Solar thermal panels come in the form of tubes or flat-plate collectors.
* In sunnier climates, solar thermal can sometimes be used to contribute hot water for underfloor heating or to feed radiators.
* You may need planning permission for solar panels in some areas.

Wind Power

* Wind turbines are best suited to more exposed rural areas where wind velocity will be adequate enough to justify investment in a turbine. They are seldom suitable for urban areas, although turbines are increasingly being used at the tops of contemporary skyscrapers.
* Carefully research the suitability of a site for a wind turbine by commissioning a consultant and investigating potential wind speeds.
* Mini-turbines tacked on to the roofs of homes usually prove inadequate. Wind turbines generally need to be mounted on stand-alone masts of sufficient scale and size to generate a meaningful amount of electricity.
* Wind turbines may be particularly well suited to small rural communities or isolated homes and farmsteads that have restricted access to grid energy.
* As with PVs, excess electricity can be sold back to the grid in some countries. Turbines also require 'inverters' to convert the power for domestic use.
* Be aware that the noise of a turbine can be distracting or disruptive if positioned very close to the home itself.
* Masts require foundations and may need planning permission.

Of the many gardens, it's the rooftop vegetable plot that perhaps provides most pleasure ... it connects what the family grow to nature and what they cook to the table.

BRICAULT HOUSE, LOS ANGELES, CA, USA

BRICAULT DESIGN

The home that Paul and Cicek Bricault have created for themselves is a house of many gardens. Set among the streets of Venice Beach, Los Angeles, the Bricault House offers a choice of green zones, each with a very different purpose.

A courtyard garden to one side of the house offers the Bricaults' two young children a green and secure play area, as well as connecting strongly to the interior of the house. Up on the roof, the Bricaults have a modest meadow as well as a highly productive vegetable garden. And perhaps most dramatically of all, one section of the house is clad in a vertical sedum garden, creating a living screen. It is, at least for the moment, a more than unusual proposition for residential Los Angeles, although an idea that is increasingly capturing the imagination of architects and designers internationally.

'I always say to my wife that the green wall is our third child,' says Paul Bricault, a professor at the University of Southern California and early stage venture capital consultant. 'We are constantly tweaking the walls and adjusting the irrigation. We are now much more finely attuned to their needs and I do like to think of the house as a living organism, particularly as a lot of it really is living and breathing.'

The house itself has evolved and unfurled over the years, like some kind of exotic animal. It began life as a small bungalow, dated 1911, facing the street but has expanded into the rear section of its site with a large addition made by a developer in the late 1990s. Some years after buying the house, with their second child on the way, the Bricaults began to think about extending again while also adopting a highly eco-conscious approach to the reinvention of the building.

The family enlisted the help of Paul's brother, Marc Bricault, an architectural designer based in Vancouver. Marc Bricault's redesign and extension of the house – which doubled the total floor area - introduced a whole series of eco sensitive measures, including the green roof and vertical gardens, while also establishing connections between inside and out and maximizing natural light.

Insulation standards are high, energy needs are low and to avoid air conditioning Marc Bricault used a natural venting system that draws in cool air from the open doorways along the 'breezeway', which connects to the courtyard garden, and expels hot air from a skylight at the summit of a dramatic stairwell that ascends through the house and up to the roof garden. A significant array of solar panels was installed on the roof, which provide nearly all of the electricity used by the family.

Yet, of the many gardens, it's the rooftop vegetable plot that perhaps provides most pleasure, serving so many different purposes at one and the same time. As he works on the roof with his children it reminds Paul Bricault of his own childhood, when he helped his father tend their own backyard plot. More than this, it connects what the family grow to nature and to what they cook for the table.

'The kids come up with me every weekend and they are happy to eat the food that comes from the roof,' says Paul Bricault. 'If I buy something from the vegetable store, they will turn their noses up at it. But if I say that it came from the roof their eyes light up, they get excited and they want to try it. It has dramatically extended their vegetable portfolio and it's been great for us to eat what we grow.'

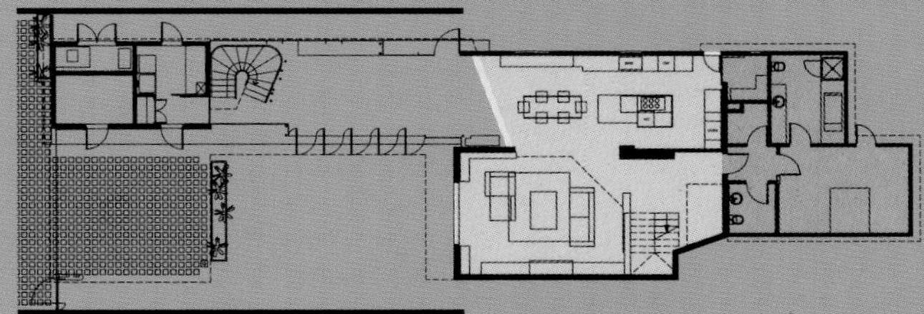

Ground floor

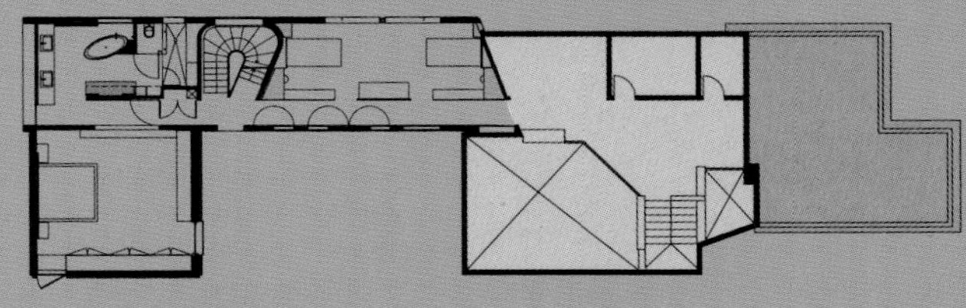

Upper floor

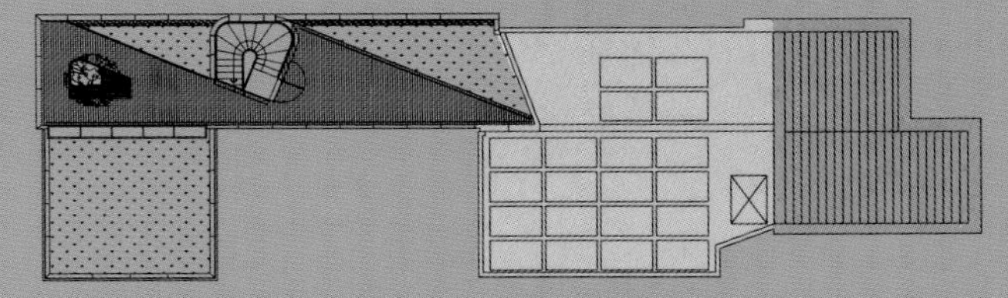

Roof level

Pages 214–17 The long 'breezeway' connects the new and older parts of the house. It plays a key role in ventilating the house in the warmer months. Cool air is drawn in through the open glass doors, and then hot air is drawn up through the stairwell at the end of the 'breezeway' and vented through a skylight at the summit.

Above and opposite The key living spaces of the house are largely open-plan, with easy access down to the new 'breezeway'. Light timber floors and white walls help light to circulate, while French windows and a variety of glazing help draw in sunlight from many different directions, including a large picture window over the library's bookshelves.

Opposite and below Features such as the staircase and the glass tiles in the master bathroom enrich the character and aesthetic delight of the house. The stairs are a bespoke design by Marc Bricault, while the glass tiles are a modest homage to Pierre Chareau's Maison de Verre in Paris. A glimpse of the green wall from the landing helps enhance the link between the house and its many gardens.

This page and opposite
The vertical garden and roof garden form part of the eco-aware strategy that runs throughout the design of the house. Electricity is provided by photovoltaic panels on the roof; these supply most of the Bricaults' needs. There is also a small meadow garden on the roof, plus a vegetable garden. 'Now my kids come up to the garden with me every weekend and plant things,' says Paul Bricault. 'They like to eat the food that comes from the roof, and the great thing about being a gardener in California is that you can be pretty inept and still succeed.'

'It's very easy to drive past it and not notice the house at all, which is an achievement in itself. When you are inside the building the windows become a lens for viewing the landscape – that's the intention.'

GLEN VIEW, HALESWORTH, SUFFOLK, UK

JAMES GORST ARCHITECTS

The creative balancing act between designing a country home that is beautiful, enticing and welcoming on the one hand yet discreetly placed within the landscape on the other is not always an easy one. However, Glen View in rural Suffolk manages both and a great deal more on a modest budget, including low energy use and a good degree of self-sufficiency.

Architect James Gorst – who has a house in the area himself – designed the building by drawing inspiration from the discreet, crafted quality of black-painted Suffolk barns, as well as a warm, almost Scandinavian aesthetic.

'Formally it is quite complex, but I was inspired by that vernacular tradition and it does sit quietly in the landscape,' says Gorst. 'It's very easy to drive past it and not notice the house at all, which is an achievement in itself. When you are inside the building the windows become a lens for viewing the landscape – that's the intention.'

Rather than placing the house across the site, which is surrounded by fields and farmland, Gorst pushed the building into the modestly sloping landscape lengthways. This minimizes the impact of the façade from the nearby road and avoids the traditional pattern of a front and back garden. Bedrooms are placed to the rear, pushed into the slope, while the volume opens up to the front within an open-plan seating, dining and kitchen area, with large picture windows making the most of the farmland vista.

The house was built by local craftsmen using a prefabricated larch frame, which went up on site very quickly. The cladding is also in larch from sustainable sources, while high-spec glazing is complemented by layers of insulation made of recycled paper, creating a high-quality thermal envelope.

Glen View has its own water supply from a dedicated well, while the main living area features an effective wood-burning stove. General heating is provided by a ground-source heat pump, with pipework buried under the garden alongside the house.

'We used a ground-source heat pump as it's one of the alternative energy sources that really seems to work and is cost-effective,' Gorst says. 'The underfloor heating stops the house getting damp in the winter, so it's an ideal form of energy. The only thing that the house takes from the grid is electricity.'

In the main living spaces, oak panelling on the walls helps to soften the interiors with the warm textures of the crafted natural grain. The floors are in recycled slate tiles, while the bespoke kitchen was also made by local joiners.

Glen View represented something of a challenge to both architect and client in creating a tailored and sustainable rural home within a modest budget. The building passes its own test with flying colours.

Pages 224–27 The house is positioned discreetly within the landscape. Rather than spreading itself across the breadth of the site, like many traditional English homes with clear front and back gardens, the building is pushed lengthways into the gentle gradient of the modest hillside. 'The house works in contrast to the gradient of the slope and cuts into the land at the back, where we have the low-ceilinged bedrooms,' says Gorst. 'It then rises up at the front, where we have the main open-plan living spaces within a considerable volume.'

Left and below Oak-veneered ply panels add a sense of crafted character and warmth to the open-plan kitchen, dining and seating area, as does the reclaimed nineteenth-century slate floor. Picture and slot windows frame views of the surrounding countryside. 'When you are inside the building, the windows become lenses for viewing the landscape,' says Gorst.

The house benefits from solar gain in winter and uses natural cross-ventilation in summer, while the green roof and thick insulation panels help to insulate the building, all cutting down on energy use.

MARSHALL HOUSE, PHILLIP ISLAND, VIC., AUSTRALIA

BARRIE MARSHALL/ DENTON CORKER MARSHALL

Out on Phillip Island, the locals call Barrie Marshall's weekend home 'the bunker'. The architect seems content with the tag, as it sums up the kind of low-key, low-impact house he planned and built and which is now concealed within the oceanfront landscape on the southern shore of this resort island two hours east of Melbourne. Set among dunes and grassland, the house's presence is only hinted at by the angled chimney protruding through the green roof.

'I can hardly claim that my whole life is built around environmental concerns, but here I was very conscious of the fact that the house is in a great setting,' says Marshall, a principal at one of Australia's leading architectural practices, Denton Corker Marshall. 'We are in a rural area on a curving, crescent bay with a sandy beach and it's a place that's great for swimming, fishing and surfing. There's nothing worse than going to a beautiful place like that and looking back from the beach and seeing a two-storey monstrosity of a house looking as though it owns the whole beach.'

Marshall has been coming to Phillip Island since he was a child. He and his wife and grown-up daughter shared a timber house on the more sheltered northern shore, overlooking Western Port bay, for many years. Then they came across a 10-acre plot on the more rugged and remote southern shore, looking out to the ocean and without another house in sight.

'The small bay that we are on has only three houses sitting on it,' says Marshall. 'I suppose I really surprised myself by designing a house that was as low-key as I could make it. The rocks on the headland are black, dark stones and I wanted the house to be this slab of dark grey concrete echoing the stones but sitting right among the landscape.'

Marshall levelled out a patch of ground for the house, edging into a hillock of dune and grassland to one side. The low-slung, one-storey house was built on site as a thin rectangle facing the ocean, and then earth was carried over the roof, greening it with scrub. To the rear Marshall created a large enclosed courtyard with concrete walls and a slim driveway entrance, as well as hidden garaging sunken into the dunes to one side. The outside of these walls was piled up with dirt mounds and again grassed over.

The simple floor plan runs parallel to the ocean, allowing for a sequence of three bedrooms, a kitchen/dining room and a living room. The kitchen sits at the centre of the house, with a modest indent in the façade creating a small protected veranda to the ocean side. A modest glass pavilion pushes out from the kitchen into the courtyard to the rear, creating a sunroom capturing the northern sunlight.

Windows are punched into the concrete façade to focus and frame views of the ocean, while openings to the rear, including the low sequence of windows in the hallway, are more about drawing in sunlight. The house benefits from solar gain in winter and uses natural cross-ventilation in summer, while the green roof and thick insulation panels help to insulate the building, all cutting down on energy use.

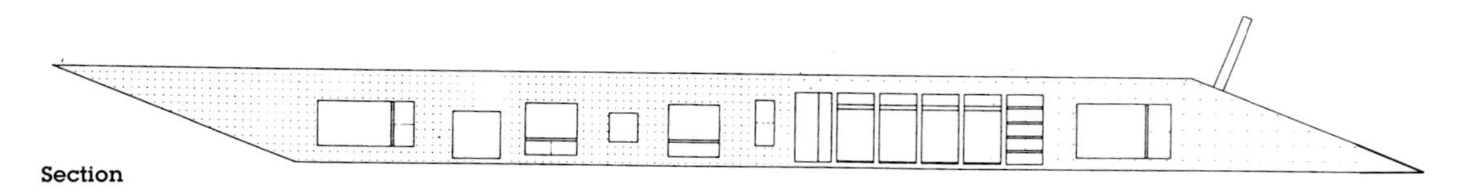

Section

Ground floor

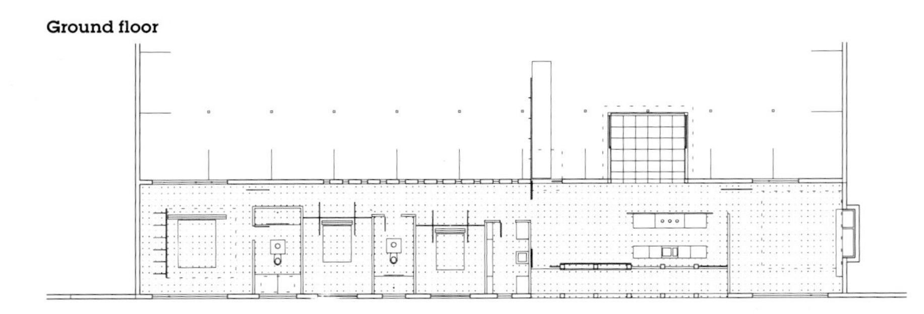

Pages 230–33 A modest access road leads into a grassed courtyard concealed in the dunes, while the house itself – facing the ocean – appears almost invisible when viewed from any distance away. The grass, dunes and scrub appear to overwhelm and consume the house, and even the tell-tale chimney flue is partially shrouded by a shrub.

Pages 234–37 The interiors are simple and minimalist, with an emphasis on the raw character of the materials, the quality of natural light and – of course – the ocean views. 'Here we wanted to keep everything to an absolute minimum, partly because it is a weekend house and not somewhere that we live every day,' says Marshall. 'When you look out, the view becomes a painting or photograph framed by the dark concrete.'

'It was a conscious decision to try and source locally as much as we could, as well as using local builders.'

PETIT BAYLE, TARN-ET-GARONNE, FRANCE

VICKY THORNTON WITH JEF SMITH OF MELD ARCHITECTURE

It was the gift of a piece of land in a quiet, scenic backwater of south-western France that spurred on Vicky Thornton's dreams of building her own unique and green rural escape. The British architect already knew this part of Tarn-et-Garonne intimately, as her parents kept a period farmhouse here for twenty years. When they finally decided to sell up, they passed the baton by giving their daughter a slice of land that originally belonged with the farmhouse. This was enough to fire Thornton's imagination.

The resulting house is a striking contemporary haven in a landscape of rolling countryside, winding lanes and the small hilltop villages that are dotted throughout the area. Perched on a hillside, the two-storey building opens up to the landscape, with living spaces on the upper level to maximize the views and leading out on to a dramatic elevated terrace overlooking the gentle green valley below.

The sloping site is around 100 by 250 feet, with a pine plantation behind the house and green meadow to the front. It made sense to work with the slope and push the building into it, so you enter the rear of the building at the top of the hill and find yourself on the upper level, made of a timber frame and clad in chestnut wood. The lower ground level anchors the house to the hill and is made of local limestone recycled from a demolished building.

'It was always the idea that the house would project out into the landscape and take advantage of the amazing views,' Thornton says. 'But we were also really interested in using local materials so that it would sit well in its surroundings and refer back to local buildings – especially farm buildings.'

The upper level is devoted to the master bedroom and a large, open-plan living, dining and kitchen area leading out to the elevated terrace. The interiors are dominated by walls made of Oriented Strand Board (OSB), formed from compacted woodchip, which gives a simple and rustic look to the spaces, contrasting with the crisp white dining table and other furniture.

Downstairs, the feeling is rather different, with the thick stone walls coated in lime render. Here there are two further bedrooms, as well as a large utility room, complete with two large tanks to hold harvested rainwater for irrigation and for flushing the toilets.

As well as rainwater harvesting, the house has a sedum roof along with roof-mounted solar thermal panels for providing hot water. Natural cross-ventilation avoids the need for air conditioning, even in the summer. The materials for building the house – including the stone and chestnut cladding – were all sourced locally to cut down on transport miles.

'It was a conscious decision to try and source locally as much as we could, as well as using local builders,' Thornton says. 'The windows were made in Moissac, fifteen minutes away, and the timber frame for the upper level was also made locally. I think it is important to contribute to the local economy when you are doing something like this.'

This is a modern house with real character, but it is also highly practical and designed to be low-maintenance – an important factor for a holiday home. Shutters on both levels can close up the house when it is not in use and protect it from storms, while the finishes are purposefully rugged and hard-wearing.

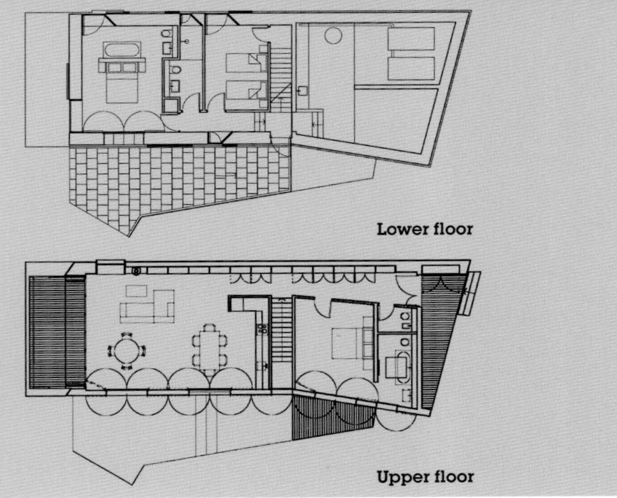

Pages 238–41 With its combination of local stone and timber, and with its sensitivity to the landscape, Petit Bayle has the feel of a contemporary version of a bank barn pushed into the hillside. 'It does tie itself to its surroundings, but at the same time it doesn't look like anything else in the area,' says co-designer Jef Smith. 'I do like the idea of an object alone in the landscape and was really pleased with the way that the house engages with the land.'

Opposite and this page The raw textures of OSB, made from compacted woodchip, provide a base note for the interiors on the upper level, but splashes of colour enliven spaces such as the kitchen and fireplace while key pieces of furniture also introduce brighter notes. The open-plan living spaces on the upper level expand out – via folding glass doors – to the elevated terrace. As well as providing space to sit out, the terrace offers panoramic views of the valley spread out in front of Petit Bayle.

Above Thornton used local materials and builders to create Petit Bayle. 'They subcontracted out some elements like the masonry work, but the builders did a good job and built the house very well,' says Thornton. 'They cared about it and wanted it to be right.'

Above 'I really wanted the opportunity to build my own house, which is fantastic for an architect,' says Thornton. 'And I also wanted to keep my ties with this region and spend as much time in this part of France as I can.'

With the mountains towering around them and ski runs alongside, it is an extraordinary spot for this timber-framed, larch-coated eco-friendly home.

STROLZ HOUSE, LECH, AUSTRIA

DIETRICH UNTERTRIFALLER ARCHITEKTEN

Having project-managed the construction of the local biomass plant, you might expect Marcell Strolz to build a green family home. In fact, he has done that and more, creating a striking contemporary house on the edge of the village of Lech. With the mountains towering around them and ski runs alongside, it is an extraordinary spot for this timber-framed, larch-coated eco-friendly home.

Building in Lech can be something of a challenge, as no second homes are allowed in this small community in the Arlberg mountains. Architecture in a modern style can also be contentious. Then there are factors like the extreme conditions and avalanche danger. Strolz and his wife, Uli, had to take all of this into account when they decided to build their own house, which they share with their two young children.

However, as Strolz grew up in Lech, he knows the area intimately and volunteers as part of the avalanche-protection team for the village. When he found a plot of land just on the edge of the 'red zone' he was well aware of the avalanche risks and factored them into the design of his family's new home. 'It is very difficult to get land here to build a house so we were lucky to have the opportunity. There is some steelwork, as well as the timber frame, to strengthen the house and we also have a series of sliding wooden shutters to protect the building,' says Strolz. These wooden shutters can be closed off to seal the windows at times of avalanche risk or during the annual 'snow roll' from the nearby Omesberg, which passes close by after a controlled explosion.

The house is gently pushed into the hillside, with a large basement area holding a garage, boot room, storage areas and utility spaces as well as the entrance hall. Flexibility was a key aspect of the design, with two separate apartments – one for rental and one for a nanny – integrated into the outline of the building along with the family's own living space. The main living area is open-plan, leading out to the veranda, with bedrooms and Strolz's study on the floor above.

The building was designed by Helmut Dietrich of Dietrich Untertrifaller Architekten, while Strolz was closely involved throughout, both in managing the build and getting involved in construction. He has worked on a number of engineering projects in the region; his biomass plant, opened in 1999, is fed by woodchip from the area's forestry industry and now supplies hot water for domestic use for most of the village.

Naturally, his own new house is linked to the biomass plant, which feeds the underfloor heating. Strolz also installed photovoltaic solar panels on the roof that are cleared of snow during the winter and make the most of the sun. The layers of snow on the roof proper add to the high levels of insulation keeping the house warm in winter. The timber for the frame and larch cladding was procured from sustainable sources.

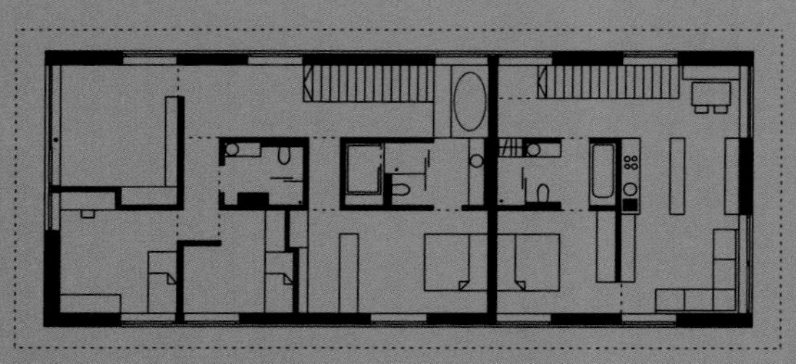

Upper floor

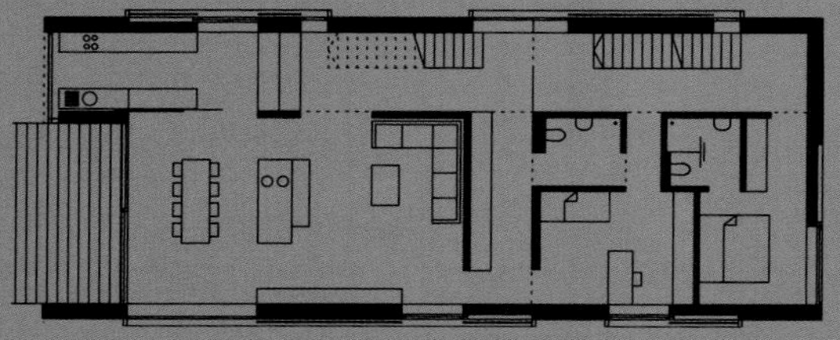

Middle floor

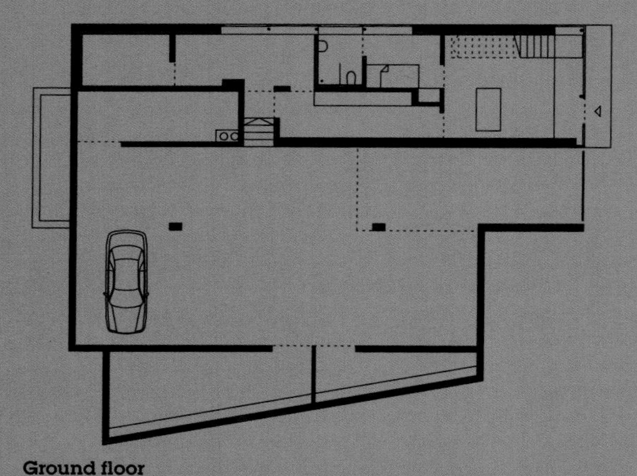

Ground floor

Pages 246–49 Set against the backdrop of the towering mountains and on the edge of the village, the house may seem somewhat vulnerable to the elements. Yet it was carefully designed to be robust, practical and characterful. When closed, it assumes a crisp outline similar to that of a barn.

Left and opposite In the winter, the snow piles up around the house to a considerable depth, and the runs outside offer a procession of skiers gliding by in the distance. The kitchen window is the one window in the house not protected by a wooden shutter but does feature specially toughened safety glass to protect against avalanche risk.

Opposite and above One of the key features of the design is its flexibility and the way it can adapt to the evolving needs of a growing family. 'Flexibility is important,' says architect Helmut Dietrich. 'The situations that families might find themselves in do change very quickly. There is also a great built-in respect for the environment in this region. Here it was the connections with nature that interested me most, and the views of the mountains and the valley.'

Directory of Architects

Abalos+Sentkiewicz Arquitectos
Gran Via 16, 3C
28013Madrid, Spain
+ 34 915 228 792
www.abalos-sentkiewicz.com

assembledge+
6363 Wilshire Boulevard, #401
Los Angeles, CA 90048, USA
+ 1 323 951 0045
www.assembledge.com

Boltshauser Architekten AG
Dubsstrasse 45
8003 Zurich, Switzerland
+ 41 (0) 43 311 1949
www.boltshauser.info

Bricault Design
1395 Odlum Drive
Vancouver
British Columbia V5L 3M1,
Canada
+ 1 604 739 9730
www.bricault.ca

Denton Corker Marshall Pty Ltd
49 Exhibition Street
Melbourne, Victoria 8000,
Australia
+ 61 3 9012 3600
www.dentoncorkermarshall.com.au

Design King Company
Unit 102, 21 Alberta Street
Sydney, New South Wales 2000,
Australia
+ 61 9 261 3062
www.designking.com.au

Dietrich Untertrifaller Architekten
Arlbergstrasse 117
A-6900 Bregenz, Austria
+ 43 (0) 5574 78888-0
www.dietrich.untertrifaller.com

James Gorst Architects
The House of Detention
Clerkenwell Close
London EC1R 0AS, UK
+ 44 (0) 207 336 7140
www.jamesgorstarchitects.com

James Russell Architect
116 Brookes Street
Fortitude Valley 4006, Brisbane,
Queensland, Australia
+ 61 7 3257 0818
www.jamesrussellarchitect.com.au

John Friedman
Alice Kimm Architects
701 East 3rd Street, Suite 300
Los Angeles, CA 90013, USA
+ 1 213 253 4740
www.jfak.net

John Pardey Architects
Beck Farm Studio
St Leonard's Road
Lymington,
Hampshire SO41 5SR, UK
+ 44 (0) 1590 626 465
www.johnpardeyarchitects.com

Kim Utzon Arkitekter
Nordre Toldbod 23
1259 Copenhagen K,
Denmark
+ 45 3393 4334
www.utzon-arkitekter.dk

Kraus Schönberg Architects
42C Halliford Street
London N1 3EJ, UK
+ 44 (0) 207 354 8113
www.kraus-schoenberg.com

Lehm Ton Erde Baukunst GmbH (Martin Rauch)
Quadernstrasse 7
6824 Schlins, Austria
+ 43 (0) 5524 8327
www.lehmtonerde.at

Marcio Kogan
Alameda Tiête, 505
Cerqueira César
São Paulo 01417-020, Brazil
+ 55 11 3081 3522

Marmol Radziner
12210 Nebraska Avenue
Los Angeles, CA 90025, USA
+ 1 310 826 6222
www.marmol-radziner.com

Meld Architecture
302 Davina House
137–149 Goswell Road
London EC1V 7ET, UK
+ 44 (0) 207 490 5249
www.meldarchitecture.com

Glenn Murcutt
176A Raglan Street
Mosman
Sydney, New South Wales 2088,
Australia

Philip Lutz Architektur ZT-GmbH
Am Ruggbach 9
6911 Lochau,
Austria
+ 43 5574 468 01
www.philiplutz.at

Robertson & Hindmarsh Architects Pty Ltd
26 Station Street
Naremburn,
New South Wales 2065,
Australia
+ 61 2 9439 7779
www.robertsonandhindmarsh.com.au

Rudy Ricciotti Architecte
17, bd. Victor Hugo
83150 Bandol, France
+33 (0) 4 94 29 52 61
www.rudyricciotti.com

Sebastian Mariscal Studio
320 West Ash Street, #103
San Diego, CA 92101, USA
+ 1 619 702 3100

Studio Arthur Casas
Rua Itápolis 818
São Paulo SP 01245-000,
Brazil
+ 55 11 2182 7500
www.arthurcasas.com

Studio KO
7 rue Geoffrey L'Angevin
75004 Paris, France
+ 33 (0) 1 42 71 13 92
www.studioko.fr

Techentin Buckingham Architecture, Inc.
201 S. Santa Fe Avenue, No. 102
Los Angeles, CA 90012, USA
+ 1 213 437 0171
www.techbuckarch.com

Tony Owen Partners
Unit 2, 5–11 Queen Street
Chippendale
Sydney, New South Wales 2008,
Australia
+ 61 2 9698 2900
www.tonyowen.com.au

Index

ALPHARETTA
Atlanta-Fulton Public Library